# ASK WENDY

# ASK WENDY

*Straight-Up Advice for All the Drama in Your Life*

WENDY WILLIAMS

wm
WILLIAM MORROW
*An Imprint of* HarperCollins*Publishers*

HarperCollins books may be purchased for educational, business, or sales promotional use. For information please e-mail the Special Markets Department at SPSales@harpercollins.com.

A hardcover edition of this book was published in 2013 by William Morrow, an imprint of HarperCollins Publishers.

FIRST WILLIAM MORROW PAPERBACK EDITION PUBLISHED 2014.

*Designed by Lisa Stokes*

Library of Congress Cataloging-in-Publication Data has been applied for.

ISBN 978-0-06-226839-6

14 15 16 17 18 OV/RRD 10 9 8 7 6 5 4 3 2 1

This book is dedicated to my handsome, insightful husband, Kevin—my partner, the love of my life. I also dedicate this to my beautiful, curious son, Kevin. Thank you both for adding so much to my life and for allowing me the room to soar to such great heights.

# CONTENTS

# ASK WENDY

# INTRODUCTION

Go on . . . ask me anything. That's what people have been doing for twenty-five years on the radio and on my TV talk show. "Ask Wendy" has become more than just a popular advice segment . . . it's become my calling card. Wherever I go, aside from the usual "How you doin'? You're so much prettier/thinner in person!" I get served up a question: "Wendy, my mother . . ." "Wendy, my boyfriend . . ." "Wendy, what would you do . . ." I always say I'm just a woman from New Jersey who is looking at the front door of fifty. I have no fancy degree to qualify me as an expert on relationships. But what I do have is a load of baggage. There are many things in life I've done absolutely wrong that I am eager to cop to and hopefully help someone through my example. In my life, I've met so many people with interesting situations and I've seen people make some pretty stupid mistakes. I don't need to be burned by the fire to know to stay away from it.

I've always thought "Ask Wendy" needed to be a book. There's a lot of drama out there and only so much advice I can give in under three minutes. Often on the show, I don't have the opportunity to get my full thought out before we have to go to commercial break. I continue talking to the person—but the public isn't hearing it. What you hear is a sound bite, and often it's just the tip of the iceberg. I want to go deeper. I want to really give someone who is confused, lost, or freaked out a solution they can use. I want to get to the heart of the issue: What's really going on here?

So I was excited to sit down with some of your toughest problems and grapple with them. I also put out the word to my loyal audience: "Send me your hardest relationship questions!" The questions flooded in, questions ranging from Work Drama ("Help! My boss is a psycho!") to Sex Drama ("My boyfriend bit me!") to everything in between. I read each and every one of these letters and e-mails—some a dozen times over. Then I thought, "What would I do if I were in your shoes? What is the underlying issue here? What are the repercussions?"

If you ask my opinion, I'm going to give it to you straight, no chaser. Each relationship you handle differently: How you handle your boyfriend is not how you handle your father. What you say to your best girlfriend you might never tell your mom. Which is why I organized my advice into chapters based on where the drama is coming from. That way, when an issue arises with your boss at work or your husband at home, you know what page to turn to. People have felt comfy telling me their drama for many years, and the older I get, the more drama I seem to attract! There's something about me that puts people at ease to show their crazy.

But I have faith in people; I believe you have the power to solve your own problems. You just need a kick in the butt. If you haven't figured it out already, I am all about getting your shit together. I don't believe that any situation is hopeless. As long as you've got a breath in your body and a brain in your head, you can move forward and fix things.

Every life has drama. If someone tells you their relationships are drama-free, they are full of it. I find that love them as we might, not everyone in our lives wishes the best for us. Some people like the drama; they love your mess and they feed off your misery. It's these folks you need to steer clear of. Not sure who they are? I am. I can smell 'em a mile away. I'll teach you how to weed out the toxic types, sort the friends from the frenemies, and keep the family ties from choking you. I want you to be proactive. Don't wait till drama rings your doorbell. Read this book, see what's out there, and be prepared to handle it.

I'd like you to walk away wiser. I'd like you to get a laugh out of some of the crazy shit people deal with ("My husband has a flatulence problem . . ."; "My boyfriend told my mom I'm great in bed . . ."). I'd like you to feel empowered to find your own answers and smooth out the bumps in your life. Sometimes I think you know the answer before you ask the question—you just need someone to verbalize what's already in your heart and head. That would be me—and I am happy to take on that role.

So ask away . . .

with love & gratitude,

Wendy Williams

## HOT TOPIC
### Is Drama Good for You?

I know we'd all prefer to live drama-free lives, but drama isn't *always* a bad thing:

- It helps you define what you want/don't want in your life, i.e., a crappy dead-end job or a cheating boyfriend.

- It encourages you to be proactive: "I'm fed up and I'm not gonna take it anymore!"

- It makes you appreciate what really matters: loving, supportive people in your life and your own personal happiness.

- It lets you reexamine and reevaluate: What am I doing? Why am I doing it?

- It moves you forward, rather than standing still. If you've got aggravation, you're going to have to do something about it.

# CHAPTER 1

# GIRLFRIEND DRAMA

Admittedly, I am not the easiest girlfriend to get along with—and that's because I believe that we outgrow our friendships. I feel that there is a season and a reason for every friend in our lives. Friendships fade. I've seen this happen time and time again. The girls who were so important to me in elementary school in New Jersey virtually vanished from my life in high school. Could I have tried harder to maintain these friendships? Could I have clung to them, tooth and nail? Sure. But I'm a practical person. I understand that people grow up and grow apart.

When I got to college in Boston, many of my NJ friendships dissipated. I didn't have tons of money or time to spend hours on the phone catching up, or to take a flight or a bus back and forth. When I was working day and night to build my career, some people in my life whom I was close with got tired of my schedule. And when I got married and had a kid, there were a few single ladies who couldn't handle it. I had left the team. In all these cases, we stopped fitting into each other's lives.

I can see some of you shaking your heads at me. You're not going to ask me to join your book club or knitting circle any day soon! You're the girl who considers her friendships to be the most precious relationships in her life. If that works for you . . . fine. But if your girlfriend is giving you grief (and from the sound of some of the messages in this chapter, many of them are!), then you have my permission to cut the ties. I want you to understand that your well-being, your dreams, your sanity, trumps any girlfriend's bitching and moaning. Do you hear that? You asked me . . . so I told you. I believe in breaking up with your BFF.

**My friend is always one-upping me, telling me how much better she is and how I should be more like her. Basically . . . she makes me feel like crap sometimes.**

Well, if you enjoy feeling like crap, you're all good. If not, time to sit this girlfriend down and have a conversation. Be very direct: "Since when did we become competitors instead of friends?" Tell her you miss the way things used to be between you: supportive, nonjudgmental, fun. You did not sign up to be her emotional punching bag! Tell her you're not sure how or why the dynamic changed, but you feel she is criticizing you unfairly. Do not, I repeat, do not, expect her to take this well. Especially since she thinks she's the greatest thing since Spanx. You can try and soften the blow by saying the reason you are telling her this is that you want your friendship to last. If she denies her disses—or worse, insists you deserve them— you have a choice: Keep taking it or get walking. I don't know about you, but I hate junk in the trunk, crap in my closet, and frenemies in my life. What's the point? All of the above just weigh you down.

I know it's hard to let go of people/things that have been with you forever. But like I said: Sometimes it's time to call it a day. Case in point: I once had a friend who I knew from the party scene. We kissed boys, and we had fun.

For a while, neither of us had a boyfriend. Then I met Kevin, and what do you think happened? All of a sudden I didn't have as much time for my girlfriend. I felt conflicted. I wanted to spend time with her, but I had this brand-new boyfriend and I really really, really liked him.

What really changed things was when my friend ended up sleeping with Kevin's friend. Of course the friend told Kevin—as boys will do—and he was not very impressed by the company of women I was keeping. Kevin and I continued to date, but he always kind of looked at her sideways every time she came to our house. When we got married and had a baby, there really was no room in our lives for her anymore. It amazed me how opposite we had become, how our priorities had shifted. I didn't feel like we knew each other anymore—that part of my life was behind me. We'll always have the memories, but I moved on.

Maybe you should do the same. But if you choose to give your friend another chance, then don't let her next insult slide. Stop her in her tracks. When she says something negative or does something hurtful, do not, I repeat, do not let her get away with it. Make her clarify or take it back. You are not a doormat, so don't let her walk all over you.

## HOT TOPIC
### Can We Talk?

Whenever you have something difficult to say to a friend, there's a right way and a wrong way to do it. I recommend you do it face-to-face—no texts, no phones, no IMing. Man up (or in this case *woman*-up). Break it to her gently but in person. I know confrontation freaks most people out, but you need to be one hundred percent honest about what's bothering you or the relationship will fall apart. The way to get things resolved is to talk it out.

**Spill it**. Keeping your hurt and anger bottled up is a recipe for disaster. You'll only wind up making nasty little remarks (what I call the "back at ya," passive-aggressive approach) or worse, exploding in a major fit. The last thing you want in your friendship is a smackdown. Instead, calmly and clearly express how you feel. If you do so in a kind and loving way, your friend won't feel as threatened.

**Don't point a finger** (or give her the finger!). Try to make this about how you feel—not how she screwed up. Avoid saying things like "You always . . ." or "You did this and that . . ." Instead try, "When you said these jeans make my ass look huge, it really hurt my feelings . . ."

**Prepare for the worst**. Your friend may deny all, storm off, or even tell you that you got it all wrong. No one likes to be called out. Just remember: A real friend won't flee. She'll want to work things out with you. Be prepared for the friendship to be over. All you can do is speak your truth. You are not responsible for how your friend handles what you have to say. At the very best, you two will work it out and keep an eye on each other. On the other side of that, the friendship might have expired.

• • • • • • • • • • • • • • • • • • • • • • • • • • • • • • • • • • • •

**My college roommate just got a divorce and has nowhere to go. She asked if she could move in with me and my boyfriend till she gets back on her feet. I live in a tiny studio apartment. How do I nicely tell her no?**

There is no nice way because she doesn't want to hear the word *no*. She's feeling desperate, which is why she put you in this very awkward situation. I get that you want to be there for her—so be there. Take her to lunch and let her vent; help her find a new apartment; lend her a couple of bucks to help tide her over. There are many ways you can be a tried-and-true friend without letting her crash on your couch. This isn't college anymore. You have another person in your life who is part of the decision-making process, and he is not gonna appreciate your old roomie sulking around his place. Be kind and let her down easy. And remember that sometimes the best way to help someone stand on their own two feet is to give them a gentle nudge out the door.

## HOT TOPIC

### Polite Ways to Take a Pass

As women, we tend to be "people pleasers," putting others' happiness before our own. This can lead to resentment and stress—and who needs more of that in her life? Learn to say no to things you have no time, energy, or desire to do. Be polite but firm; don't let yourself get manipulated or guilted into it. Otherwise you'll just wind up bitching to me about it!

SCENARIO 1: Your boss calls during dinner and wants to go over work details.

HOW TO HANDLE IT: "I'm sorry, but we're in the middle of eating. Can I please call you back when we're done?"

HOW NOT TO HANDLE IT: "My hours are nine to five. See ya in the morning."

SCENARIO 2: A class mom asks if you would bake cupcakes for tomorrow's holiday party.

HOW TO HANDLE IT: "Gee, I'm sorry . . . my oven is broken. Maybe next time!" or buy a box of Entenmann's.

HOW NOT TO HANDLE IT: "Do I look like Martha Stewart to you? No way!"

SCENARIO 3: A friend asks if you wouldn't mind taking care of her cat while she's on vacation for a week.

HOW TO HANDLE IT: "Aw, I wish I could! My hubby is violently allergic to cats!"

HOW NOT TO HANDLE IT: "You think I want to change a litter box while you lie on a beach in St. Barts? Screw you!"

SCENARIO 4: Your neighbors invite you to a party at their place.

HOW TO HANDLE IT: "That's so kind of you. Unfortunately, we have previous plans that night."

HOW NOT TO HANDLE IT: "Can I see your guest list and get back to you on that?"

SCENARIO 5: Your kid's ballet school calls to ask for a donation to its annual fund.

HOW TO HANDLE IT: "I'd love to give, but it's a tough year for us. Maybe when things get a little better financially . . ."

HOW NOT TO HANDLE IT: "You've got some nerve asking me for more money! Don't I pay you enough for dance lessons?"

. . . . . . . . . . . . . . . . . . . . . . . . . . . . . . . . . . .

**I am only having two bridesmaids in my wedding and I have two sisters, so I can't ask my best friend to be one. She's going to be seriously pissed. How do I handle it?**

Simple: You don't need to do this to her or to yourself. What's wrong with a lopsided wedding party? So he has two groomsmen and you have three bridesmaids . . . big deal. When it comes to weddings, I say avoid drama at all costs. For this reason, I'm a Justice of the Peace Girl, ya know? But if you MUST have equal girls/guys, ask your fiancé if he has a third friend who could step in and be a groomsman. Or create a special position for your friend: Ask her to lead the toast, read a poem during the ceremony, even lead the conga line. Tell her how much you appreciate her and want her to be part of your Big Day. Like I always say, if she's a real friend, she'll be cool with it.

**My friend told me she hates my boyfriend and thinks he's a loser. We've known each other since we were four years old (we're twenty-seven now), and she thinks she knows what's good for me.**

Maybe she does and maybe she doesn't. Unless she has a damned good reason to hate on this dude (i.e., he stole money out of her purse or groped her when your back was turned), I say she's overstepping her boundaries. What would make her say something like that? Maybe she's jealous that someone is "stealing" you away from her. Or maybe she's been unlucky in love in the past and is projecting her man-hating 'tude on your relationship. Often when someone criticizes you for your choices, they're really saying they're unhappy with their own. So you need to get to the bottom of this. Time for a sit-down. Tell your friend you realize she doesn't want you to get hurt, but in this case—unless she has strong evidence to the contrary—your boyfriend is not a bad guy. Explain that you are committed to him, and that this relationship is here to stay—so she has to make peace with it. If she can't, then tell her to at least keep her opinions to herself unless you ask for them. Tell her you'd love her seal of approval, but if she can't give it, that's okay, too. She doesn't have to love him . . . that's your job.

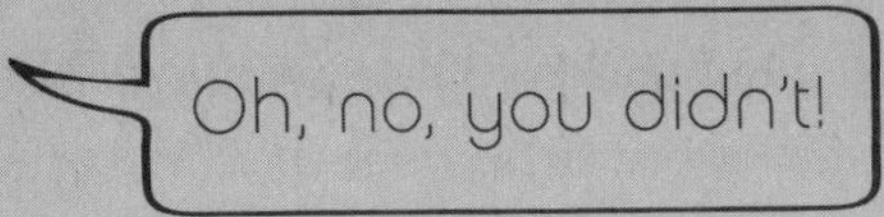


SEX SECRET

**I got drunk and slept with my best friend's brother. She's always warned me that he's a total player who sleeps around, and I know she will FREAK if she finds out. What should I do?**

I can't believe I am saying this, but I feel like it's coming from a positive place: Don't tell her. The dirty deed has been done (hope it was worth it!), and unless you plan on a repeat performance (are you seriously into this guy when you're sober?), let it go. Why risk hurting your friendship, especially when she "warned you" to stay far, far away from her skanky sib? If she told you not to go there, you should have respected her wishes. But what's done is done. Now all you can do is damage control. I would talk to the guy and make sure this is something that will never be spoken of again.

**Every time I go to lunch or dinner with my friend, she stiffs me with the check. I've paid a few times. But I'm not made of money.**

Again, communication. People talk it! How 'bout next time you get a little cash, you take her to lunch and tell her why this will be the *last* time you pick up the tab? Tell her you love her, but you're not made of money, ya know? That's probably her issue as well: She doesn't have the money but wants to hang with you. Suggest a bunch of stuff you can do that's free: Watch a movie at home or go take a walk in the park. By stiffing you with the bill, she's basically "borrowing" money from you without the intention of paying it back. This in my book is a big no-no. Whenever you "lend" your friend money for a meal, it makes you resent her—or else you wouldn't be asking me this question, right? So stop doing it. Unless she's prepared to sign an IOU every time you go to Taco Bell, this is not a situation you should allow to continue.

**My best friend totally forgot my twenty-first birthday. I don't want gifts from my friends, but I at least want them to remember! I am really**

**hurt and feel like I should tell her off. Am I being a bitch?**

No, you are not being a bitch. But I'm glad you had a moment to remove yourself from the immediate heat and anger that I know this situation caused you. Breathe! Breathe! Now call your girlfriend, ask her over for a glass of wine, and tell her you're hurt and hope that she had a case of temporary amnesia. She'll probably feel very, very bad. She'll get you a gift (albeit a little late). I know excuses won't make you feel much better, but I gotta say it: People get busy; lives get hectic; shit happens. It's not the end of the world and you shouldn't toss out the friendship because of this one faux pas. You could have let it slide, but I get that twenty-one is a big b'day, and you hoped she would help you celebrate it. If it's important to you, then you have a right to be upset. Hopefully, she'll do right by you and put your birthday on her calendar for next year.

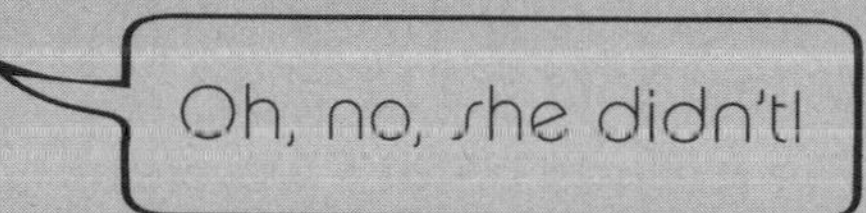


**I caught my friend making out hot and heavy with my boyfriend at a bar. I know they were doing tequila shots, but seriously?**

You're a better woman than me. You would not have been able to hold me back. I would've poured pitcher after pitcher over their heads. I would have been breaking and slapping. Drinks or no drinks, they have both betrayed you. You want my honest opinion? He's no longer your boyfriend and she's no longer your girlfriend. You can't even waste energy on screaming at this bitch because quite frankly you might find yourself ripping her head off or doing something illegal. And as far as he's concerned, kick his cheating ass to the curb. They deserve each other . . . and you deserve a shot of tequila for having to deal with these two backstabbers.

**After two years of marriage, my husband just told me he slept with one of my friends before we were engaged. He says it was just a one-night stand, but I don't think I can handle looking her in the eyes anymore!**

Why didn't he tell you? Why didn't she tell you? That to me is the issue more than this one-nighter (and I hope it was only one night!). Both of them should have spilled the beans, and not after you tied the knot. I know your husband's actions hurt you, but it's history. You got papers on each other, and nobody needs a messy divorce in this economy. So my advice is to let him off the hook. Unfortunately, she doesn't get off so easily. If it were me, I could no longer be friends with her. Period. I'd cut her off and tell her why. Friends don't lie to friends, and that's what she's done here. She should have owned up to her actions; she owed you that. By letting this much time pass without letting you know she's seen your husband naked, she's dug her own hole. Bury that bitch for good.

## HOT TOPIC
### Should You Tell?

When it comes to marriage, I am a big believer that honesty is the best policy. You are in it (hopefully!) for the long run, and keeping secrets between you breeds distrust. That said, there are certain things that should remain unsaid . . . especially if it will hurt your partner's feelings and confidence.

- **You hate his hairy back.** Most men think body hair is manly . . . so don't go telling him he looks like Cousin Itt and you wish he'd wax. Unless he's shedding on the furniture like a golden retriever, let it be.

- **You faked it last night.** Welcome to the club; we all moan and scream and don't mean it from time to time. Don't demean his sexual prowess by telling him you started to doze off during intercourse. Next time, show and tell what you need him to do.

- **You had a hot dream about your ex.** Occasionally fantasizing about an old boyfriend does not mean you want him back in your life. You're just taking a stroll down memory lane. Do not share this info with your spouse . . . ever. Not only will he feel threatened and inadequate, it might make him break out his old Little Black Book and rekindle some of his former flames as payback.

- **You think his sainted mother is a psycho-bitch.** Never say a nasty, negative word—even jokingly—about his mommy. Men hold their mothers in the highest regard. Worst-case scenario: He'll rat you out and she'll never let you live it down.

. . . . . . . . . . . . . . . . . . . . . . . . . . . . . . . . . . . .

**My roommate stole my checkbook and used it to buy stuff. I know that it's her because I recognize the handwriting on three of the checks. What should I do?**

There is nothing you can do about your checkbook. Notify your bank and put locks on everything in your apartment. Get a police report together and take it to your landlord and tell him you want to break the lease.

You are living with a thief, and you need to get your ass out of there ASAP. If she tries to backpedal or beg your forgiveness, don't listen. A thief is never sorry that she stole—only that she got caught red-handed. I know you may feel bad because you once liked this girl, but she's betrayed your trust, raided your bank account, and God knows what else you might find missing. Run don't walk and never look back.

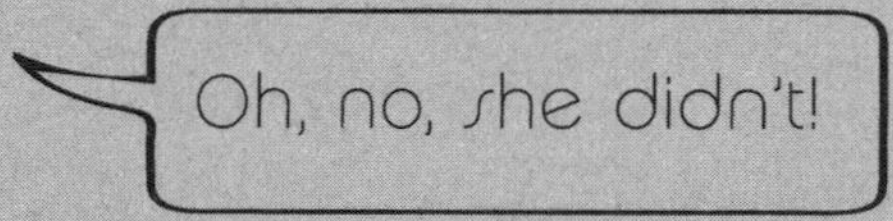


**My so-called friend told my fiancé he shouldn't marry me—one of my other friends overheard her. She thinks I'm "too needy." What the hell is up with that?**

Your so-called friend is also your so-called enemy . . . apparently. So she needs to be cut from your camp right now. Done. Erase her from your phone. Erase her from your memory. Now. How dare she try to sabotage your wedding and your life like this? If she had concerns that you weren't right for each other, she should have come to you with them—not your man. This is no well-meaning buddy looking out for you! Go to your fiancé immediately and let him know that nothing in the world is more important to you than loving him and becoming his missus. Your commitment to him is unwavering and screw her! Hopefully, he feels the same about you and would never allow some negative words from a totally unreliable source to sway his opinions.

**Two of my best friends just told me they were lesbians. I am so not. I like my boy toys and I have no idea what to say to them or how to act around them now that they are together.**

How should you act? Like you've always acted! I know the news was a shocker to you, and it's not your cup of tea . . . but that's okay. Embrace what they are and who they are—they're not asking you for anything more. Act normal and ask questions if you need to. Be honest if you're feeling awkward or uncomfortable when you're hanging out as a trio. (They might be into PDAs or going to gay clubs.) They obviously trust you and respect you enough to share this news with you, so be the supportive, compassionate friend you always were. Straight or gay, nothing has changed in your friendship.

## My friend borrowed my BMW and totaled it. She says she has no money to pay for the damages. What should I do?

As long as she's okay and uninjured . . . you have a right to be majorly pissed about this. The very least your friend could have done is offer you the last cent she has. Or pay you back on a ten-year installment plan. Or sell her gold fillings to fix the taillight. But NADA? Not acceptable. Prepare to lose this friendship (especially if you have to sue her). Prepare to buy yourself a new car. Prepare for your insurance premium to go up. It sucks, but lesson learned: Never let someone who is not on your insurance drive your car. If the Allstate man isn't covering her, you shouldn't let her take the wheel. Put on your big-girl panties and take responsibility for your actions.

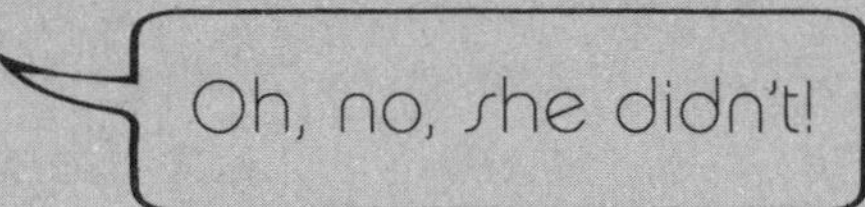


**My maid of honor got trashed at my wedding and threw up on the dance floor. I really feel like I should say something . . .**

The wedding is over and done. You had a great time. She obviously had a great time (maybe too much of one!). Maybe the stress of the Big Day just got to her? No harm done. You're still married. Let it go. The embarrassment of puking in public is painful enough. Unless your friend has a history of overdoing the alcohol (in which case, an intervention might be in order), it's better not to bring it up (pun intended).

## TOO CLOSE QUARTERS

**My college roommate is banging her boyfriend every night in our dorm room. They don't seem to care if I'm two feet away, and earplugs aren't working.**

In another lifetime, I would have told you that you need to go out and find someone to bang, too. (Payback is a bitch!) But I'm more responsible than that now, so I will give you my grown-woman response. Your roommate is very inconsiderate. I know what it's like living in a dorm and this is a very precarious situation that goes on all the time. Sit that roomie down and set her straight. You both live in that tiny space, and she can't go about her business when you're trying to study for your calculus exam. If she apologizes and wants to work out a fair schedule (i.e., you go to the library for an hour while they use the facilities), then fine. But if the sexual antics continue, I'd recommend you go to your RA and see if maybe you can move rooms. This is not to say this won't happen again with another roommate. The important thing to do is set some boundaries from day one. And if the earplugs aren't doing it, invest in a white noise machine . . .

**Ugh, my roommate is a pig! She leaves her dirty dishes in the sink, her skanky underwear on the floor, and last week I found one of her tampons floating in the toilet. How can I get her to clean up her act?**

I feel your pain. I am always telling my teenage son to stop leaving his dirty laundry on the floor for me to pick up. And I cannot stand how his bedroom always smells like raw ass. The boy is clean. He takes showers. He's just messy and farts a lot!

So, get ready: It's time for a roommate throwdown. You're going to tell your roommate you want to talk to her, meet out in the common area of your apartment like the living room, and lay down the law. Here's how I would do it: "Girl, there are a couple things I just want to talk to you about. It's about the filth and the funk. You leave dirty dishes in the sink. You do it once, you do it twice. I get it: We're all busy. We're all rushing. But it looks nasty and it doesn't smell nice. Then there's the underwear. If you don't respect yourself enough to pick up your panties, then at least kick them under the bed where I can't see them . . ." Don't let her make excuses. (She will try.) Tell her to get bins, hooks, a laundry bag, whatever. If you have to, tack a chore schedule to the fridge so she doesn't forget what she needs to do. There is only one way to deal with someone so sloppy: Make her clean up her act. If she doesn't, threaten to take a pic of the mess and e-mail it to the dude she's crushing on. He won't be ringing your doorbell any day soon.

## WENDY'S FINAL WORD
### Tips to Avoiding Girlfriend Drama

- **Return clothes, shoes, and handbags in the same condition you borrowed them.** Please do it within forty-eight hours, and dry-clean if necessary.

- **Do not borrow money or men.** Period.

- **Avoid letting problems pile up.** You know I'm a talker. I believe if you've got an issue with me, or I've got an issue with you, someone needs to put it on the table. Keeping your mouth shut because you don't want to rock the boat will only make matters worse.

- **Don't make promises you can't keep.** The surefire way to piss someone off—especially a close friend—is to flake out on them. Be honest if you can't make dinner plans or hold her hand at the dentist's office. If you say yes—then backpedal—it's gonna be ugly.

- **Refuse to take the bait.** If a girlfriend is purposely doing or saying things to aggravate, then don't let her. Simple as that. Ignore it. The people who know you the best are the ones best equipped to push your buttons.

- **Do unto others.** You should treat your friends the way you want to be treated. What you put out there, you get back tenfold. I really, truly believe that.

# CHAPTER 2

# MAN DRAMA

My big mistake in the man department has always been thinking I needed/wanted certain things in a partner. I had a mental checklist. I saw my mom and dad married more than fifty-five years and I created this very idealistic plan of what a good relationship looked like. When I was younger, I thought I should find a guy at my socioeconomic level and everything would be perfect. But that doesn't always happen. Sometimes the Harvard-educated girl meets the plumber and falls madly in love with him. You've got to open your eyes to the prize! And that prize doesn't always reflect what you and your family *thought* they wanted for you. Sometimes love comes out of nowhere and surprises you.

Coming from a solid middle-class background, I had these expectations of the type of man I would wind up with—a Barack Obama or Colin Powell type. A successful, polished, driven, well-educated man. As a result, I wound up dating a lot of gay men. (My gaydar was pretty lousy!) I had a marriage that lasted less than six months, and I got involved with men I knew were all wrong for me. After all that, my prince turned out to be a guy from the wrong side of the tracks. Big Kevin never graduated high school, but he's taught me a thing or two! The most important lesson I've learned is that struggle is something that builds character. If you're handed everything on a plate, you don't have a chance to do for yourself.

I will say, quite honestly, that our relationship has been through hard times. My husband cheated on me while I was pregnant with our son, and I put up with a lot during that time. A lot (see "Should You Forgive a Cheater?" box page 60). But it's a relationship that is worth fighting for—and I can only say that now because I've been through the fire.

So here's my final thought before I tackle all your man drama: Love will find a way. Shit happens, but somehow love always finds a way.

**I've been in a relationship for three years and we're both twenty-two and talking about getting married. But one thing is bugging me: My boyfriend stays in contact with his baby mama. Should I let him?**

It's not a matter of you *letting* him. Dealing with a relationship like this takes great maturity from all parties involved, and someone has got to lead by example. That someone might as well be you. Give him the space that he needs to maintain a relationship with his baby's mother. We're not talking about them being friends or lovers. We're talking about him being a responsible coparent. Being a parent is the most important and most difficult job in the world (this I know from experience), so I give him some credit for this. If you are going to move forward in your relationship, then this "blended family" is part of it.

Now, here's the sadder-but-wiser Wendy talkin': Keep an eye on them. It's one thing if he wants to be a part of his kid's life and keep tabs. It's entirely another if he still has feelings for his ex and is playing you for a fool. I know three years is a long time to be with someone, but be very sure before you tie the knot that you want to be married to a guy with this much baggage. Quite frankly, I think you are biting off a lot by even being involved with a man who's already a daddy. When I was in my twenties, I had a rule: Never fall for a guy if he has kids. You're young; you have your whole life ahead of you! You're practically a kid yourself, and you want to deal with *his* kid? Okay, 'nuf said. But if you have doubts, don't be afraid to break things off with him. It's a lot easier now than when you have a ring on your finger.

## HOT TOPIC

### When Should You Stay Friends with an Ex?

Every relationship and every breakup is unique—so there isn't one general "rule" I can give here. If the guy's an abusive, obnoxious, pompous ass and the breakup was hostile . . . do not give him the time of day. Move on. Delete him from your contact list. If your heart is broken and the very thought of him makes you a hysterical wreck . . . sever all contact. But if you find yourself in any of these situations, you might want to give it a try:

- **You were friends first.** Okay, the romance didn't work. You realize you're a better duo sans the sex. As long as there's no conflict involved, and you truly care about each other, a platonic relationship (again!) is a possibility.

- **You work together.** For the sake of keeping things civil on the work front, it's probably worth it. The last thing you want is for your boss to think you can't function anymore as a team—and hand one or both of you pink slips.

- **You have the same social circle.** Meaning no matter what you do, you're going to see each other when you're hanging out. Might as well keep things cordial between you. You also don't want to put your other friends in the uncomfortable position of choosing sides.

**My ex texted me for a booty call, and I kind of want to see him. Neither one of us is dating anyone right now. Should I?**

Yes, you should. And enjoy it! Just make sure you understand the reasons that he's your ex not your current, and that you are capable of doing this without any emotional ties. Be smart: This is not about getting back together. Hell, no! This is raw, animalistic attraction! This is scratching an itch! Don't look him in the eyes. Don't play your songs. No candlelight dinners; no cuddling and spooning. Wham, bam, thank you, ma'am. Got it? Then go get it, girl.

**My husband and I have been married eight years, and he thinks he knows everything. If I have to listen to his big mouth bragging one more time, I'm going to scream.**

You know, I've been married for fifteen years, and my husband and I have been together for nineteen. There are little things he does that drive me up the walls and things I do that piss him off. He drives like a maniac. I'm always terrified we're going to be hit by the wide body of an eighteen-wheeler driving on the Jersey Turnpike. And I like to leave the blinds open when we go to sleep. In the morning, the sun wakes me up and I am in my glory . . . while my husband pulls the pillows over his head and wants to kill me. That's what happens when you are with someone 24/7. You see each other's flaws.

But in your case, I question the bragging thing. Is he putting you down? Making you feel insecure or unworthy? Not cool, not acceptable. Has he always been kind of a blowhard, or is this something new? Is there a deeper issue? Why does he feel the need to criticize or condemn you? This is not what a loving relationship is about.

But look . . . you know your man best. You can tell if he's being serious when he says, "I'm smarter than you" or just joking. I say sit him down and have a little talk: "Honey, sometimes when you brag, it makes me feel sad or bad." Spell it out for him; maybe he's not aware that his ego is hurting his marriage. If that doesn't work, then by all means, scream. At least you'll get his attention!

## HOT TOPIC

### What Is Emotional Abuse?

I know the old saying "Sticks and stones . . ." but cruel words are not something you should accept in a relationship . . . ever. You have a right to be shown respect! Broken bones heal; emotional scars often don't. According to experts, emotional abuse is a pattern where one partner uses verbal assault, fear, or humiliation to demean the other's self-esteem and self-worth. If you're experiencing any of these signs in your relationship, you could be a victim of an abuser:

- **You're walking on eggshells.** You don't know what will set your partner off. Any little thing could make him/her see red and react.

- **You're embarrassed.** Your significant other says things to berate you in front of friends or family.

- **You feel stupid.** Or inadequate. Or insecure. Whenever you talk to your partner, he/she puts you down, criticizing everything from the way you look to how you cook dinner.

- **You feel bullied.** Your partner tries to control everything you do and say because he or she is "smarter/better" than you.

If you recognize these signs, then don't wait another minute. Get help. Seek out support or counseling. The American Psychological Association (APA) Locator (http://locator.apa.org) can help you find someone in your area. Remember that you have done nothing wrong to cause this situation. The issue is with the abuser.

**My best friend from high school hinted that he wants to take things to the next level, translation: hook up. I'm not really interested, but I don't want to ruin the friendship.**

Then tell him exactly that. Nothing cutesy like "I think you're really hot, but . . ." Make it crystal clear: "I really value your friendship, and I don't want to muddy the waters by jumping into bed with you." Straight talk makes for straight understanding. If he's not mature enough to understand that, then he doesn't deserve your friendship. Even if you put this behind you for now, realize there will forever be sexual tension in your relationship. He threw it out there, and he can't take it back. He's gonna wait for that one moment when you're feeling vulnerable (bad day at work; too many drinks) to swoop in and change your mind. Just be ready. Be sure of where you stand on this, and don't let him pressure, manipulate, or guilt you into doing something you don't want to do.

**Why is every hot guy I am interested in gay? I feel like I should give up and become a nun!**

I know it feels that way sometimes, but I swear, every unattached guy on the planet is not gay, and you shouldn't give up hope. When I was single, finding Mr. Right had nothing to do with the population out there. There were guys everywhere! That was never my problem. My problem was knowing what I wanted out of life—that's what was holding me back from attracting the right people. Part of knowing what you want comes with age and experience. My parents have been married for fifty-five years and still counting. I grew up in the suburbs of New Jersey, where family (and okay, maybe food!) was everything. So I figured out I didn't want to compromise: I wanted both, a family and a successful career. And that's when my hubby, Kevin, came along. He was a giver, not a taker. He was supportive of my already big radio career and not threatened by it. He opened doors for me (and still does!).

On November 30 of 1998 we went to a justice of the peace in New Jersey. He was the singer Grace Jones's brother (I swear!), and his secretary was our witness. No family, no friends, just us. I wore a kilt skirt from Kohl's—one of those Catholic-schoolgirl "Hit Me Baby One More Time" Britney Spears getups. After we married, Kevin went back to his detail shop in Jersey City and closed it up, and I ordered Chinese food. That was that . . . and it's fifteen years later and we're still happy.

So when you're ready to really settle down and find that guy, you will. And there's nothing wrong with a few hiccups along the way. Date free; have fun. As for stacking the odds a little more in your favor, where are you hanging out? If you're doing gay bars and clubs, I'm not surprised that you're not finding many takers. Maybe try a new scene? Explore online dating? Ask friends for referrals? Keep the faith, girlfriend.

**I'm totally jonesing after this married guy in my office. I know he's always complaining how his wife is a bitch. Should I make a move?**

No, and you know something? If you do, you will pay the price and you will be sorry. It won't last, and you'll be the bad guy. First of all, "he's totally bitching about his wife" means he's totally immature. He doesn't know how to be a reasonable husband because a reasonable husband understands the rules of fighting. You don't air your dirty laundry at the office. I don't like this. I don't like his behavior, and I'll be honest: I don't like yours either. You know he's married, and you know that every relationship goes through rough waters. Don't get in the way of him trying to do what he needs to do and handle his business with his wife. Do you really want to be somebody's third wheel? You will never get your best from him. You don't deserve somebody's sloppy seconds, even if he eventually separates or divorces. So keep it moving. Tough talk, but hopefully you'll understand.

## HOT TOPIC

### Should I Fess Up to an Affair?

I want to be perfectly clear here: I don't condone cheating of any kind. I think it's nasty and low and hurtful, and it destroys lives. But I get that it happens, and not just to Hollywood celebs. People stray in a moment of weakness; it's a fact. The question is: Now what? Do you sweep it under the rug and pray your partner doesn't find out? Or do you come clean?

Hell no to coming clean! You don't confess anything. If you cheat, keep your mouth shut unless you are about to get caught. Don't get all Mother Teresa on me and say confession is good for the soul. If you cheat, you're gonna have to keep that in your vault and take it to your grave. Deny all unless there's pictorial evidence!

**I've been married for ten years, and I feel like it's the same-old same-old all the time. How can we liven things up?**

Marriage takes work; do you think that you can just sit back and things will be hot and sexy after ten years? Nuh-uh. And you can't rely on him; you gotta switch things up. You have to take it upon yourself to keep those fires lit. Use a blowtorch if you have to! I have lots of little tricks up my sleeve. I'll put on a short, tight dress and take my husband out on the town on a date night to hear a hot DJ. I'll cook something different and exotic for dinner. I'll buy a new perfume or wear my hair in a new style. You get it? Make little changes and keep him on his toes.

I also think it's great to remind yourselves of how things used to be—I can be pretty sentimental at times. Writing this book and reflecting on my fifteen years with Kevin, I used up several boxes of Kleenex. I believe in getting nostalgic. Book a vacation at the spot where you honeymooned. Go on Netflix and download the movie you saw on your first date. Remember those feelings you shared when everything was new and exciting in your relationship. Dig them up and you won't have reason to complain that the thrill is gone.

## HOT TOPIC

### Five Tips to Spice Up Your Marriage

1. **Clean up.** I don't mean the kitchen. I'm talking about grooming. No man is gonna get turned on by hairy legs, ratty sweatpants, and a dumpy/disheveled spouse. I know life is busy (especially when you have kids), but take a shower, brush your teeth, comb your hair, donate to the Salvation Army any T-shirt you have owned for ten-plus years. Make an effort to buy some new sexy lingerie and ditch the granny panties. You think he won't notice any of these things . . . but he will (and then some!).

2. **Talk.** Don't just text or e-mail. Actually have a conversation, face-to-face. The first thing to suffer in a long-term relationship is the intimacy. Make sure you make an effort to stay connected.

3. **Touch**. Hold his hand. Ruffle his hair. Massage his shoulders. I promise you that any physical connection you can initiate is the key to igniting the flames.

4. **Listen**. Remember how enthralled you were when you were first dating? How you hung on his every word? Try paying close attention when he speaks. Ask about his day; how he's feeling; what his plans are for the next few weeks. If he mentions he wants the new iPhone, then surprise him with it. (He'll be amazed not just with your generosity, but that you heard what he said.) Don't allow life to distract you from what's important: each other.

5. **Prioritize sex**. Seriously . . . schedule it in, just like you would a dentist appointment. It's THAT important. Even if you're tired, even if you're stressed, even if you're on a book deadline (Hello?), you have to take the time to nurture your sex life. Forget food; sex is the key to a man's heart. Wait till the kids go to bed, then light some candles, open a bottle of wine, break out some sex toys, and get down to business.

. . . . . . . . . . . . . . . . . . . . . . . . . . . . . . . . . . . .

**My boyfriend and I work at the same place. I got promoted and he didn't. He's pissing me off and treating me like crap. What does he want me to do? Screw up like him?**

Ahem, do I detect some hostility here? These are pretty harsh words. Is that how you see your boyfriend—a "screwup"? This is why it's not the greatest thing for a couple to work in the same place. Take it from me: I know, honey. Once upon a time, there was a cute man at work, who was eleven years older. (Make sure you are running hearts and violins in your head while you're reading this anecdote!) We were both working at radio station Kiss 98.7 in New York City. I was making well over $100,000 a year as a DJ, while he was in sales. So mostly what separated us was a whole lot of zeros in our paychecks.

We dated for about a year, and he asked me to marry him. I was twenty-eight years old and I thought marriage was something I was supposed to do at the time. So I said yes, and we planned a gigantic wedding. I probably should have seen the writing on the wall: I was throwing up at every aspect of planning the ceremony and reception, and my mother had to take over. I knew, emotionally and physically, this was wrong. If I had been smarter and braver at twenty-eight, I would have backed out. But I wasn't. And nobody picked up on my fear and terror or tried to talk me out of it. So there it was: 250 people, a yacht-club reception on a beautiful September day, and a weeklong honeymoon to Brazil. We got home, went back to work, and I was miserable. The honeymoon was literally over. We ended up separating five months into it. We had the fight of our lives, then I waited for him to go off to work (we worked different hours) so I could call a moving van and put all of his stuff in storage. I had no regrets. I was not pregnant. We owned no property together. We got involved in none of the serious stuff that was supposed to be a part of married life. But yeah, it was embarrassing.

I know everybody was whispering about us behind my back, but we still had to be coworkers. *Awkward*. At one point, the heads of the station came to me and asked, "Do you want us to fire him?" I said no, because I do have a heart. And now it's twenty years later and we're different people with different lives and I'm telling you my story.

So I get it when you tell me you're pissed at your boyfriend. I also see his side of it. You have a bigger position than him, and you have to deal with that once you get home as well as in the workplace. If you're committed to him, then try to understand what he's going through. Men need coddling. We women grow up and deal with life a lot faster than they do. They're all little boys with delicate egos. Listen to what he has to say and be kind and gentle. But if he's still hating on your situation (and there is no promotion for him in the near future), I give you permission to end it. Work romances are hard enough without someone being bitter and angry all the time. Get out before it gets ugly—like mine did. You don't need to make a movie for your coworkers.

**My husband is the breadwinner and I'm a stay-at-home mom to our two kids. He thinks that this means he gets to control how much I spend and he's always nickel-and-diming me on everything and accusing me of wasting money. He even suggests that I get an allowance. I'm not a child.**

I'm sorry, but it makes me steaming mad when men do this! No, you're not a child, and you don't deserve to be treated like one. You have one of the most important jobs ever: being a mother. Whether you're a single mother, whether you are married, whether you are living with your boyfriend, I don't care. Raising happy, healthy kids demands an incredible commitment and takes strength, dedication, and a hell of a lot of brains and heart. You work as hard as he does (probably harder). Don't let him belittle what you do. If he wants to give you a little spending money? Fine. But he doesn't need to call it an allowance—that's number one. And number two, I hate to be so harsh, girlfriend, but you need to get yourself a little part-time job, even one from home, so you can use it as leverage. It's been my experience that when a woman is able to do for herself, it solves a lot of problems. You can pay for your own manicures, shoe-shopping sprees, and the kids' toys and clothes, without asking your husband's permission.

As for the nickel-and-diming, I'm assuming you're not made privy to the inner financial workings of the household. One of the most empowering things you can do is to know how much your bills are every month and where the checkbook is—even if you are not writing the checks. You need to become a part of the finances in your house so your husband doesn't wield that power over you. And the more you understand what you have to spend and save as a family, the more you can communicate about a budget that fits both your needs.

## HOT TOPIC

### Get Over Your Jealousy!

Jealousy comes from feeling threatened. Basically, someone has something you don't or makes you feel inferior. Jealous people are insecure. The more you like and respect yourself, the less likely you are to be envious. But once you feel green with envy, how do you deal with (or derail) those feelings?

- **Make a list of your finest qualities.** Spell it out: "I'm kind. I'm considerate. I have a nice ass." I'm not kidding: Add to that list every day and remind yourself of what's on it. Work to build your self-esteem.

- **Get to the root of it.** What is making you feel jealous? Are there situations or specific people that trigger your jealousy? Why? And what can you do about it? For example, if you're jealous of a coworker getting promoted, take a class to improve your skills so you're not passed over the next time.

- **Stop comparing.** If you're always looking at others around you to see how you stack up (Is she prettier, thinner, smarter than me?), of course you're going to feel envious. Stop yourself before you start.

- **Jealousy solves nothing.** It only wrecks relationships and makes you feel angry and lousy. Take a deep breath and step back from the situation. Is it worth aggravating yourself over, or are you better off getting over it?

**My boyfriend and I are total opposites. We've been together eight months, and he's getting on my nerves. How do I get him to try some of the things that I like?**

I'm gonna be brutally honest here: Sounds like this relationship has almost expired—so much negativity in such a short period of time. I mean if you're total opposites, what attracted you all to each other to begin with? There is something to be said for the cliché "opposites attract," but it's the things you have in common that become the very glue of the relationship. My husband and I, on the surface, couldn't be more opposite. He was raised in Brooklyn by a single mom and he lived in the projects. He did not graduate from college, and given his neighborhood, he could have easily been dead by now. I, on the other hand, am from the Jersey burbs, and I experienced lots of the best things in life materially as well as emotionally.

But the glue that keeps us together is, we both want the same things. We want what's best for our son, and what's best for each other. Kevin is my manager. Does he get on my nerves sometimes? You betcha. But the bigger picture is, I love him and I believe in us.

How do you get your boyfriend to do more of what you like to do? You ask him. Relationships are about give-

and-take, and your feelings for each other should count enough that each of you bends and is flexible for the other. If he can't do that, then it's just not meant to be.

**My significant other made a lame excuse about not taking me to his parents' house for Thanksgiving. We've been dating a year and he never wants me to meet them. What's up with that?**

Maybe he's super sensitive about his family. Maybe they're a mess? His uncle has no teeth. His mother talks with a lisp. His father has one leg. His sister is in prison for drug smuggling. And so on and so on. The point is, you don't know what's up on the home front, and this may not be about you. Or maybe it is . . . meeting the parents takes the relationship to a whole new level. It suddenly turns things serious, and maybe he's not ready.

My big question is, why haven't you had this conversation with *him*? Have you ever actually told him how you feel ("I really want to meet your family") and asked why he's keeping you far, far away from the kinfolk? You don't need a holiday to make this happen—sometimes holidays are too fraught with pressure and drama. Just pick a plain ol' weeknight and meet his parents for dinner someplace casual. If he still says no, he better have a good reason.

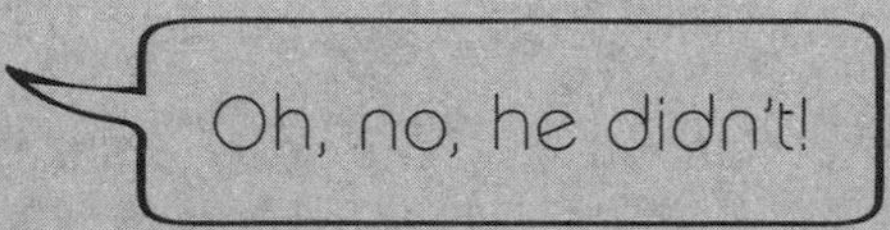


**My boyfriend told my mother I am wild in bed. I am mortified. He said he was joking, but my mom is totally freaked. She said she thinks I should dump his ass.**

So do I! What a jerk. Why would he say something like that? All kinds of secrets are forged between two people in a loving, healthy relationship, and you don't expect those secrets to be blurted out in front of anyone. Not your mother, your sister, your coworker. Nobody! Is he serious? This shows not only immaturity but also insensitivity. How does he think your mother now feels? Ick! Ya know I asked my husband about this one. He happened to walk into the room while I was reading it out loud and he agreed: Dump his ass. You do what you want, but we say, "Dump his ass."

## HOT TOPIC
### How to Apologize When You Screw Up

Everyone does things in life they're sorry for. Me? I'm sorry I ate the entire deli section at ShopRite. Genoa salami is my Kryptonite and I can feel it traveling right now to my hips and my butt. I don't say it's easy to admit that you're wrong, but sometimes you just have to bite the bullet and beg forgiveness. A few of my tips:

- **Mean it.** Don't just mumble, "I'm sorry," really be sincere. Say you know what you did was a mistake and you wish you could take it back. Be honest and genuine.

- **Own up to it.** Whatever you did, take full responsibility. Right any wrongs (if possible) and don't make excuses. You made your bed, now lie in it.

- **Do better.** Promise that next time, you won't make the same god-awful mistake. You'll be smarter and more sensitive. You'll never forget this indiscretion and you'll learn from it.

And if all of the above fails, bribery isn't a bad option. Personally, I prefer a heartfelt eye-to-eye conversation and a kiss. I can buy my own jewelry and handbags. Just look me in the eye and tell me you love me. Now we're all good.

• • • • • • • • • • • • • • • • • • • • • • • • • • • • • • • • • • • •

**My fiancé and his friend like to smoke pot, and do it whenever they hang out, which is every weekend. He says it's fun, but I'm worried he's got a problem.**

I would think you'd be more worried he'd get caught. Hopefully, he's smoking responsibly. Let's face facts: Weed is virtually legal all over the place, and where it's not legal, people want it to be legal. I happen to be a person who does not want marijuana legalized, but I'm not hating on the weed-head. It's something to you and it's something to me, but it's nothing to most people. So stop being so corny and get with the program. What you should be concerned with is: Where does he get his weed from? Is he up on the Boulevard? Standing with someone leaning into his Camaro while he buys a nickel bag? Obviously, he realizes the legal ramifications, and that's what you should be concerned about at the end of the day. It's something that could get him fired from his job. Watch his behavior carefully when he smokes. Does he want to punch his fist through glass because he feels sudden anger? Does he get inappropriately flirtatious with women? Does he turn into an ass and bitch out waiters and waitresses at restaurants? Does he forget his manners? I say if it's no to all of those things, then chill out.

Some people smoke weed like other people have a glass of white wine at the end of a long day. It is not right, but it's a fact.

If you're engaged, it means you intend to make this man your lifelong partner and coprovider as well as father to your children. So you need to decide what is important to you. This pot problem didn't just pop up. He's been smoking weed since the day you met him. So what's really bugging you here? Are you concerned about moving ahead with the relationship? With what kind of parent he'll be? Have a conversation with him and let him know how you feel. Hopefully, the pot isn't as important to him as you are.

**I had a one-night stand with this guy and he got me pregnant. Now he refuses to help or deal with his son. He says it's my problem, not his. How can I get him to take responsibility?**

The short answer is, take his ass to court and get everything you need from him. Show no mercy. Since he has no feelings about you or his son, you have no feelings about hanging him out to dry. And the next time you're having sex with some guy, make sure that he uses a condom and you use some form of birth control as well. It's pretty inconvenient to find yourself in this situation. Be smart and don't let it happen to you again. If you're going to have a fling, cover your ass. I'm not judging ('cause we've all been there before) . . . just saying.

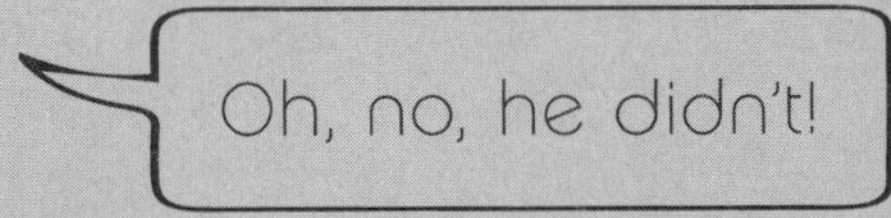


**My husband is always commenting on how hot the babysitter is. Should I be worried?**

Yes, and you should also fire the babysitter. I know there are many women reading this right now saying, "Wendy, you are too insecure!" Yeah? Well, I watch a lot of Lifetime movies. Did y'all never see *The Hand That Rocks the Cradle*? But I do think your husband has caused this situation (and her unemployment). How dare he mention this to you at all! Why is he noticing some other woman's hotness? I hope he's not saying this to you to belittle you, because that is just wrong. I say kick her to the curb and find somebody that looks like Mrs. Garrett from *The Facts of Life*. She's spunky and good with kids.

## HOT TOPIC
### Should You Forgive a Cheater?

I get a lot of questions from both men and women about this. As I mentioned earlier in this chapter, I've had my own personal experience with a cheating husband. What I can tell you is this: It hurts. It hurts like hell. It was something I wasn't sure I could get past—especially given the fact that it happened more than once during the time I was pregnant. I had several miscarriages before I was finally able to get pregnant with Little Kev. We had an honest talk with our doctor and we all agreed: no sex till the baby was born. It was just too risky. During that time, Big Kevin cheated on me. He cheated with a woman who was younger than me. She was single and knew he was married, but I don't blame her. I blame him. He's the one who knew what he had to lose.

I didn't find out until after my son was born. He was maybe two months old when I overheard my husband on the phone with the other woman. It actually woke me up. My parents were staying in the house with us in Jersey, so they got to witness firsthand the door slammings and all that mess. We had some very volatile fights at that time. But then it occurred to me: I was better with him than without him. And despite what went down, I loved him and still love him. So we stayed together and we worked it out. We are better for it. We've been married now for fifteen years and we've been together for nineteen years. We are a team—spiritually, lovingly, business-wise, and in raising our son. But I had to learn to trust again. I had to stop looking in his telephone and searching his pockets. I had to let it go.

If you're not sure if you can forgive and forget, ask yourself the following:

- **What were the circumstances?** Was it a onetime indiscretion at his brother's bachelor party in Vegas, or has he been making regular booty calls to your neighbor down the block? I know people say once a cheater, always a cheater, but I do believe sometimes guys have a momentary lapse of sanity and do something they regret.

- **Did he tell you?** Or did you have to snoop, spy, or pry it out of him? I was in shock when I discovered my husband on the phone. If he'd maybe come clean before I caught him red-handed, I would have been pissed—but maybe not homicidal.

- **Is he really sorry?** Is he begging, crying, scraping on his hands and knees for your forgiveness? Does he see the error of his ways, or is he trying to deny it or pass the blame?

- **Can you ever trust him again?** Without trust, there is no relationship. You can't spend every waking moment wondering if he's screwing around behind your back. You need to really think this one through: Is your relationship beyond repair?

- **Can you make lemonade out of lemons?** By this, I mean can your relationship learn and grow from this incident. Strangely enough, this is what I found to be true. Kevin and I are better as a couple having survived and worked on this together. But both people have to be willing to roll up their sleeves and do what it takes. There has to be real, honest communication between you going forward.

**My man told me I need to lose weight. I am so upset! I thought he loved me the way I am.**

No, he apparently loves you the way you *were*. I'm just so hurt for you that this actually came out of his face. I don't believe that gaining weight means you're not beautiful and desirable. But some men . . . they just blurt out whatever fleeting idea crosses their minds. If it'd been me, I would have immediately started crying. I would've run into the bathroom and bawled. I'm talking tough in this book, but you have to know I'm very sensitive to this. I have been fighting fat all of my life because I love food. Honestly, I feel your pain!

But you know this isn't all about him. It's really about you. Put aside the fact that this was a totally insensitive comment. How do you feel about your weight? Do you think you need to lose a few pounds? I know, girlfriend. I know it's easier said than done. And I know this comment hurt because you feel bad about your size. But it's your business, and you can handle it. You can get to the gym and you can make healthy eating choices. If you want it, it's possible. Trust me—take control and the scales won't matter anymore.

Don't let him get away with saying this to you ever again, especially if, like me, weight is your Achilles' heel. Wonder how much he'd like it if you pointed out his bald spot?

## WENDY'S FINAL WORD

### Rules for Avoiding Man Drama

Men and women are very different creatures. (That whole Venus and Mars thing is true.) They think a certain way and we think a certain way, and the only way to avoid arguments in my opinion is to do the following:

- **Keep it to yourself.** If you do have to share your relationship woes, choose one person and assume that person will tell at least one more even if you have sworn them to secrecy. Heck, I'm probably reading my husband one of your stories right now! But the issue is between the two of you—not your kids, your family, your coworkers. Nothing pisses a guy off more than you complaining to your girlfriends about the size of his penis. Anything between you two is not for publication, you hear me? Unless there is abuse involved, in which case I do recommend you reach out and tell so you can get help.

- **Stop trying to change him.** It's like beating your head against a wall. The more you tell him to pick up his dirty laundry off the floor, the more he thinks you're a nag. Instead, lead by example. If he sees greatness in you, he's gonna want to do all he can to hold on to you. Be the kind of woman who makes him want to rise to the occasion and be the best that he can be.

- **Don't share finances unless you're married.** Don't pay for his phone. Don't let him use your credit to get a Visa or a car or even a pair of sneakers. Don't cosign on his student loans. Don't do it. Don't do it. Don't do it. He is not your husband or your responsibility. You are only trying him out. Once you're married, you can do what you want.

- **Cook something.** I know many of you are going to hate me for it, but this is a biggie. I cook three times a week, and I must tell you, I am no Iron Chef. On a scale of one to ten, I'm a five. I do have my particular deliciosos that they love. I make the best pancake and sausage and egg breakfast on Sunday mornings. I cook a terrific lasagna for a black girl from Jersey. I make a mean olive-oil chicken and some damn fine tacos. Just ask Kevin: He'll sing the praises of my hot-dog-and-beans casserole. I'm not a fancy cook, but my husband and my son love what I make. They appreciate it. Do not underestimate the power of lovin' from the oven.

- **Stay hot.** Men are visual creatures. You may have graduated from MIT and be the best nurse the OR has. But, honey, that don't matter if those extra twenty pounds have been sitting on your butt since the birth of your third child! You have to try to keep up your appearance. Put on lipstick and mascara.

Wear something cute that shows off your cleavage. I am telling you that your man notices. If you feel sexy about yourself, it keeps him on his toes. Which brings me to . . .

- **Don't get lazy.** This goes for more than just your appearance. It goes for the way you did things then and do them now. You don't want your guy to wake up one day and wonder, "Who the hell are you?" We can only do the best that we can, but if you cooked every day when you were first married and you haven't touched a stove in years, you sold a false relationship. Same goes for sex: I'm not saying you have to bang-bang-bang ten times a week like it used to be. They say the average couple has sex two and a half times a week. That should be your minimum. Don't get lazy with laughter—remember to smile and joke together. Make sure you continue to make out on a regular basis, too. Not just a peck on the cheek—a real French kiss that involves tongue. Don't get lax with the wax: Make sure you keep your privates neat and tidy. Always think of what attracted him to you in the first place and don't lose it.

# CHAPTER 3

# DATING DRAMA

I was about twenty-nine years old when I met my husband, Kevin. He was twenty-two, and it was the spring—April 6 to be exact. I was working at a roller rink in New Jersey. I was a popular deejay at the time, and I was always getting hired to host parties and events. I was single, and it was just another night. Random. Guys were always passing me their telephone numbers and I never really paid much attention to them. But there was something about Kevin. He was there with a bunch of his boys from Brooklyn. He owned a business at the time, a hair salon, and he was also a party promoter. He had one of his friends give me his phone number. It turns out I drove a Pathfinder at the time and so did he, and the note came with a little message: *Let's drive our Pathfinders in the mud.* I thought that was so cute. But I didn't call right away.

Two days later, I was about to get off my shift at the radio station, and I noticed this telephone number at the bottom of my bag. Guess who? I called it and said, "Look, I get off at six. Here's the address of the radio station. I'm hungry. Take me for something to eat." Straight and to the point. He came and picked me up, and oh my God, I fell in love with him. He had the most beautiful smile, and when I got into his car, he smelled *so* good. He had on a nice outfit—gritty street clothes, only a Brooklyn boy would have on. I like a tough guy and that's that.

We went to Brooklyn to close up his salon, then he took me by his apartment. It looked like a dive, and he had nothing in the fridge. I remember I wanted to get out of there quickly. I told him to take me to Houlihan's on the Hudson River. We drank Heinekens out of the bottle. We ate chicken nuggets and cheeseburgers and I licked my fingers. He thought I was going to ask him to take me to get lobster and shrimp and all that fancy stuff! Not this girl!

After that, we went back to my apartment. Yes, on the first date! I broke my own rule. We talked all night long and we've been together ever since.

So what's the moral of this story? You never know when love is gonna come along and bite you in the ass. Date. Date a lot. Date guys you wouldn't normally think would be your type. I've always believed that there is someone (or multiple someones) out there for all of us.

**I feel like I'm always playing the game with the guys I meet. Do I always have to pretend to be something I'm not to get a guy to like me?**

No, you don't—you should never be fake. Like I said, I put on no airs when I went on my first date with Kevin. If he was expecting a high-powered radio personality, he was in for a rude awakening. I sashayed my way to the parking lot of Houlihan's in jeans and Timberland work boots. And that was that. That was me. So I say be who you are on a first date. I know it's important to impress, but please be normal. Don't let this guy get used to a girl that you are faking it to be. It's tough to keep up that guise, and one day—when you let your guard down and he sees the real you—it may all fall apart.

**I went on a first date with a guy and thought things went great. Obviously, he didn't since he hasn't called or e-mailed since. Should I call him?**

Do not call this guy back! He doesn't think you're the girl for a second date or a second thought, so don't you go chasing him. Have a little self-respect, girlfriend! He's not worth your time or effort. And don't feel bad that it didn't work out. Before you find your Prince Charming, you will probably be on several dates with several frogs. So be it. That's how you learn what you want and don't want in a relationship.

## QUIZ: HOW YOU DOIN'? IS HE INTO YOU?

Can't figure out if he loves you or loves you not? Answer the following honestly and check your score below.

1. When he answers your call, he says:
   a. "You again?"
   b. "I'm kind of in the middle of something. Can I call you back?"
   c. "Hey there, hot stuff!"

2. The check comes at dinner. He:
   a. Goes to the bathroom . . . and never comes back.
   b. Asks if you'd like to go dutch.
   c. Insists on paying. "It's my pleasure!"

3. On Valentine's Day, he:
   a. Sends flowers and chocolate . . . just not to you!
   b. Buys you some roses from the corner deli . . . after you call to remind him.
   c. Cooks you a romantic candlelit dinner.

4. You ask where he sees this relationship going. He:
   a. Breaks out in hives.
   b. Hems and haws.
   c. Asks you if you want to meet his parents.

5. While you're on a date, you bump into an old boyfriend. He:
   a. Asks if you two would prefer to be alone so you can catch up.
   b. Acts cool but cordial.
   c. Kisses you long and hard right under your ex's nose.

**If you answered mostly A's:** Honey, do you need a new pair of glasses? Because I think you are blind to the signs. This dude is not digging you. You need to move on to someone who appreciates your fabulousness.

**If you answered mostly B's:** I'd say he's feeling fifty-fifty. He's not sure what he wants or where you stand as a duo. So give it a little time (provided it hasn't already been five years!). If you don't see him exhibiting more of the C responses, then please, I beg of you, cut him off. The last thing you want is a wishy-washy guy who can't commit.

**If you answered mostly C's:** There's no doubt he's into you—he says and does all the right things. Just make sure he's sincere, and not trying to sell you a line. If you've been together a while and he's turning up the heat, maybe he *is* ready to take things to the next step. But if you just met last week and he's all sweet talk and PDAs, be wary. He might be trying to get into your pants, not your heart.

• • • • • • • •

**A guy told me I was a ballbuster because I refused to sleep with him on the second date. I'm no virgin, but I'm not a slut either. Am I wrong for wanting to wait?**

No. You are not. The guy was trying to call you out so you'd weaken and jump into bed with him. We women have something men want: It's called a vagina. They will always test us and try their hardest to "score." If you're not a virgin, then this news should not come as a surprise to you. As for Mr. Hot Pants, if you're not ready to get down and dirty with him, then tell him he's gotta wait. If he can't, then let him find someone who'll put out without hesitation. I hear there are plenty of them under *Whore* in the yellow pages . . .

**My friend fixed me up with her husband's brother and I found him foulmouthed and obnoxious. She**

**keeps asking me to double, but I don't want to see the guy ever again. What should I do?**

You were her friend before you were his date, so you owe it to her to be honest. I'd say something like "I'm sorry, your brother-in-law just isn't my type . . ." You don't need to tell her every little thing he did that pissed you off. If she keeps pressing you to double-date, then I'd tell her a little white lie: "I'm interested in someone else and I'd rather not." That way, you make it clear and you save face. Just also bear in mind that "never seeing this guy again" may not be in the cards. He'll likely show up one day at your friend's family events and parties. For your pal's sake, keep it as polite as possible if you cross paths.

**I've been e-mailing this guy I met online for three months. He still hasn't asked me out. What's up with that?**

Okay, girlfriend, I'm going to take a hard line, here. If he hasn't asked you out after three months of talking online, he is not going to ask you out. PERIOD. You are not at the top of his list. The way I see it, you have two possible ways to go here. The first is to call him on it: Shit or get off the pot. Ask him point-blank if he wants to get together in person. If not, that brings you to your second option. And that is MOVE ON. Disconnect your number. Do not return his e-mails. You've got better things to do than waste your time on a guy who's probably sitting in his ratty boxers, e-mailing dozens of women because he's too chicken to get out there and date.

**How do I know if a guy I meet in a bar is (a) straight, (b) single, or (c) not a psychopath? My judgment sucks.**

First of all, unlike a lot of women, I do believe you can meet a decent guy at a bar. I believe you can meet a decent guy anywhere. It's all in the energy you put out. As for poor judgment, honey, you are talking to a woman who dated a lot of gay guys by accident. It happens. Your gaydar may improve with age. Look for some signs: Are his eyebrows arched (as in plucked)? Does he swing his wrist too much when he talks? Does he sway his hips too much when he walks? Yeah, he might be gay. But it's 2013 . . . so I'm not gonna stereotype. I'm gonna tell you to go up and ask him: "Are you straight?" There is nothing inappropriate about asking a person up front if they are straight, gay, or bi. There is also nothing wrong in asking, "Are you single?" Always check for a ring or a ring mark (in case he took it off). Realize that men lie like dogs. And aside from asking them to take a polygraph test, there's really no other perfect way to tell. Don't let it hold you back. Date, flirt, put yourself out there.

**My friend wants to set me up on a blind date with her boss. I'm afraid if I don't like him, he will fire her. So should I pass?**

You should go on a date with her boss. You're both single, and she obviously thinks you might hit it off. So what's the harm? At dinner, don't include any of the usual sidebar conversations about your friend other than "It was so nice of Charlene to introduce us." And don't kiss and tell her what went on. None of her biz, even if she was the matchmaker. Don't put her in an uncomfortable situation. Whether you love him or hate him, that's not for her to know. Other than that . . . have fun!

**My college professor asked me out. He's forty-six and I think he's totally hot. But is it just too weird to date him? I am twenty-two.**

Is it weird for you to date him? Yeah, it is. He might have kids or an ex-wife or experience under his belt that you know nothing about. At twenty-two, darling dear, the world is your oyster. I remember those years. I loved being twenty-two. I had my college degree in one hand and an empty slate in the other. And I didn't want some old man telling me how to be. I barely wanted my mother and father's opinion. But this is not about me—it's about YOU. What are you like at twenty-two? Are you still twirling your hair and eating Cap'n Crunch when a Pop-Tart won't do? But if you are more mature, more able to be with a forty-six-year-old and not feel he is cramping your style, then that's your choice. I don't recommend it, but you know yourself best. Just be careful. You don't want the whole campus talking about you. You don't want the rep of the slut sleeping with her teacher.

**I've been dating this guy for two months and we haven't had sex. He hasn't even asked. Is he some kind of sexual freak? Should I be worried?**

If a guy is not leaping on you and humping your calf after two months—heck, after two days—there is a problem. And since you want sex, the problem then is with him. I don't think he's a sexual freak, I just don't think he's into you—or maybe he's gay or a virgin. It doesn't really matter. Unless you are willing to deal with either of those situations, I think you should thank him and walk away. He's done you a favor by letting you go without conflict.

**My friend's father asked me out. He's a widower. I kind of feel sorry for him and wouldn't mind having dinner or going to a movie, but what if he's really lonely?**

In my opinion, this guy is off-limits. It's just way too complicated, and a pity date is never fun. You need to pull him aside, quietly without your friend around, and explain that you are flattered but not interested. If you don't do this, this old man will continue to pursue you, and one day it will become very, very awkward. Cut everything off now and keep it moving. It's not your job to worry if he's lonely. He doesn't want a dinner companion, honey—he wants a blow job.

Oh, no, he didn't!

**I was on a date with this guy I met online. He disappeared. He said he had to take a business call outside, but he never came back. I know where he lives and works. Should I track him down and bitch him out?**

I am so angry right now, I want to track him down and bitch him out myself! But you shouldn't. In fact, what you need to do is erase everything about him from your life, including his online profile. I don't care how bad the date was, a guy does not treat a woman this way. It's just bad form. But I do have to ask: What went on? Because 50 percent of the blame is on you, girlfriend. Something made him run, and you should think long and hard about it so you don't make the same mistakes again. Did you talk about an ex? Complain about your childhood? Pick your nose? Even unconsciously, was there something that made him want to flee? Realize and revise!

## HOT TOPIC
### First-Date Faux Pas

Everyone makes mistakes, especially when you're nervous about meeting someone new. But these "oops" are unforgivable! Never, I repeat, NEVER:

- **Scope out another guy in the room.** Keep your eyes from wandering—even if a total hottie walks by.

- **Fart, burp, or blow your nose at the table.** Stifle it, sister.

- **Discuss an ex.** He doesn't want to hear how hot the sex was or how you screwed things up. Next topic!

- **Monopolize the conversation.** Allow him to get a word in and listen to what he says. Don't blab on and on about yourself. Major turnoff.

- **Text or take a phone call.** Rude, rude, rude! Unless your house is on fire, it can wait till the date is over.

- **Show up late.** It's sloppy. It says you don't care. Unless you're stuck in traffic (and you should leave extra time!), there is no excuse.

- **Pick a fight.** You may not agree with what he says, but that's no reason to start an argument. Be polite when you state your opinions—don't ball the guy out for his beliefs.

- **Spill the beans.** Save the tough conversations for when you're committed. He doesn't need to know that your father was an alcoholic, your brother is an ex-con, and you once had a nasty case of crabs.

- **Get drunk as a skunk.** Passing out in your plate or dancing on the bar is not an option, so even if you're nervous, don't overdo the alcohol. A glass or two is plenty.

.....................................

**This guy I know from my building asked me on a date and then took me to the Laundromat, where I helped him sort and fold. Is this his idea of a good time? Should I give him another shot?**

Any guy can take a girl to the movies and dinner. I've been through it a million times, and most of those dates have been pretty unmemorable. It takes a special, ballsy sort of guy to take you to a Laundromat. I have to tell you something honestly: Knowing what I know now, if a guy took me to sort and fold but we had a great conversation, I'd be cool with it. In fact, I'd be wowed because it shows he's real. Yes, you should go out with him again if you're interested. Tell him what you want to do on the date this time, but don't be a high-maintenance girl. Don't choose a fancy, overpriced restaurant. Suggest a movie and dinner at Olive Garden. Good men come in many different forms, and so far he has not indicated that he's a bad one.

**My date showed up on my doorstep wearing ripped jeans and a dirty T-shirt. He looked like he hadn't combed his hair. My roommate says I should give him another chance, but I'm scared of what he'll wear next time. Should I go out with him again?**

I just went to the mall the other day with my thirteen-year-old son and the ripped, dirty jeans were on sale there for three hundred dollars. Same goes for the "dirty" tees—the whole "distressed" look is hot right now with guys and can cost a fortune. Don't assume your date dressed like a slob. Maybe he was trying to be trendy? Honey bun, how about you go out with him again and don't judge him on what he's wearing. Judge him on the content of his character. You might find the most fantastic guy in the world whom you would have overlooked. How do I know this? I married that guy!

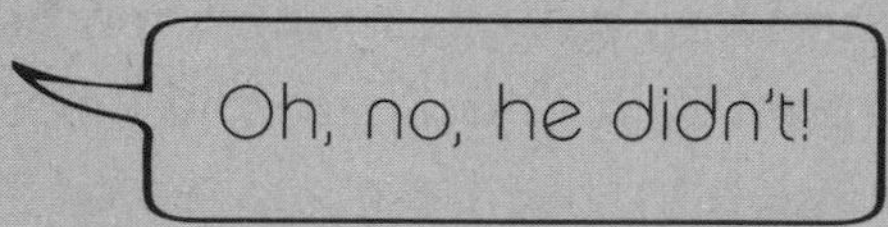


**My date bit me. I'm not talking a little nibble; I'm talking teeth marks on my neck. I kind of liked him up until now. What do I do?**

Girl! Let me tell you something, dates give love bites for a couple of reasons. (1) It turns them on and they are hoping that it turns you on, too. (2) They are trying to mark their territory so no one else messes around with you. If it's not your thing, then tell him. Chances are he'll oblige. But as someone who spent her twenties covered in hickies (that's what Dermablend is for!), I can tell you it's kinda hot when a guy bites and sucks. Why not be a little dirty? Tell him to take the bite marks to places no one will ever see, like your belly, under your boobs, your back, on your upper thighs.

**I was about to get naked with my date when he casually mentioned he has herpes. Talk about a mood killer. I really like him, but I am scared of catching it. So what do I do?**

So here's my personal story and my personal opinion on the subject: A while back I met this guy. I was an awkward fat girl from New Jersey. I fell for him hook, line, and sinker. I found myself back at his hotel room. We drank. We ate. We fooled around. It gets to the point of peeling off our clothes, and ya know what he tells me? "I have herpes." I hugged him and thanked him and I ran out of there. At least he was honest. Your guy was honest, too. Herpes doesn't kill, but it can sure make life difficult. According to the Centers for Disease Control, one in six adults between the ages of fourteen and forty-nine has genital herpes. You don't want it if you can avoid it. That said, if you do really find someone you want to be with who has it, there are things you should and shouldn't do when you have sex. You can reach out to the CDC-INFO Contact Center for more advice: 1-800-CDC-INFO (1-800-232-4636); e-mail: cdcinfo@cdc.gov.

**My date did a *Fifty Shades of Grey* on me. He bought handcuffs, whips, the whole thing. I said, "Not tonight," and now I'm freaking out. Does this mean he's a perv and should I dump him?**

Your guy probably thinks this is what ladies like, because God knows, we've all read the books! You need to talk to him. You need to say, "Look, we aren't all into handcuffs, whips, and the whole shebang." It doesn't mean he's a perv, and no you shouldn't dump him—unless he won't take no for an answer.

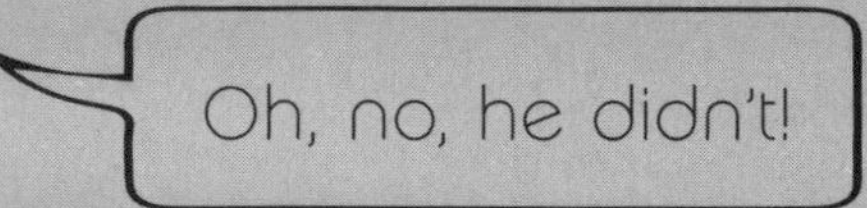


**My date asked me to come back to his apartment to introduce me to someone. I thought it was his roommate or his brother. Turns out it was his penis. He pulled down his pants and said, "Meet Big Edgar!" I was speechless. I said I had to go. Was this supposed to turn me on? He keeps calling me. Help!**

I'm assuming his penis was gigantic and he was showing it off? Even so, ewww. I find this disgusting and immature. Yes, he was trying to turn you on. He was trying to say, "Hop on and ride!" You know what I would do? I would tell him and his big dick to take a hike. He's not going to be an attentive and sensitive lover if he's already playing these childish sex games.

**I went out with this guy to a nice restaurant. He treated the waiter like crap, then he didn't tip the valet. He seemed really nice and polite to me. Should I be concerned?**

Yes, and I'm going to tell you why. First, can I tell you I am married to an overtipper? My husband tips everyone to the point that I complain, and I am a generous woman. So I see the value in it—it shows people you are grateful for and appreciative of their service. This guy was on a date with you, so he was supposed to be on his best behavior. He treated the waiter like crap. Okay, I'm turned off. Then he didn't bother to tip the valet. Okay, I'm doubly turned off. Should you be concerned? Yes. Not tipping and not treating people with respect is an indicator of a guy's home training and his thought process going forward. He might be a pompous asshole who thinks people who do menial work are beneath him. This is a lightbulb moment. I would give him one more chance (only if you insist!), but if it happens again, let that date be the last.

**I went out with this guy who seemed perfect. I should have known better. He told me he lives with his parents in the basement. He's thirty-one. What should I do?**

Why is he living there? Is either one of his parents a quadriplegic? Are they handicapped? Does someone need help up the steps? Does someone need assistance on the toilet? Does someone need to be driven to dialysis several times a week? Because I swear to you, I am not hating on a thirty-one-year-old man living with his parents if there is a valid health reason. You need to ask what's up with this. And if there isn't a good reason—and he's just a clingy mama's boy—proceed with extreme caution.

**I went to a concert with this guy and he kept farting. He pretended it wasn't him, but it totally was. Aside from that, I like him. But the gas is gross, right?**

Yeah, the gas is gross, but it happens to all of us. I drink lots and lots of water because that's what doctors recommend, and I drink it from the bottle. Do you know what that means? I am swallowing big gulps of air all day—and that makes me gassy. I got poots here and poots there. I'm farting all day. In addition I like poopy, smelly food. I love my beans. I love my spinach. None of the above is going to make my husband run screaming out the door. And I would tell you that your date's flatulence shouldn't scare you off either. Can you make a joke of it? I live with two men, and the fart jokes never grow old with guys. If it really bugs you, get him some Beano or carry matches (the sulfur smell kills the odor) or some Febreze in your purse. Don't be small-minded. The bigger picture is the guy!

## WENDY'S FINAL WORD
### How to Avoid Date Drama

Because I have been on so many dates—good, bad, and ugly—I feel I can state the following with certainty:

- **Carry cash.** Always have money for transportation home. I would take a credit card as well, because you never know if it's going to go south.

- **Dress sexy not slutty.** As mature women, we know the difference. No need to send out the wrong signal. You want to say, "I'm hot!" not "I'm horny." Unless you are.

- **Go dutch.** It's okay on a first date. I kind of like to pay my own way—it gives me a sense of power and control. But don't let it become a habit. You're investing your time and energy into this date, so he can invest some cold hard cash.

- **Don't cry.** And I'm a crier. Bunnies on commercials make me sob. I'm telling you if you cry on the first date, you will scare the bejesus out of him. Men don't know how to handle it when we cry. Not even men we've been married to for fifteen years. My husband freaks out.

- **Go easy on the makeup and perfume.** I love makeup. I think every woman should walk out of the house with at least a tinted moisturizer and lip balm. But too much of a good thing screams, "I am high maintenance. Be afraid, be very afraid."

· · · · · · · · · · · · · · · · · · · · · · · · · · · · · · · · · · · · ·

# CHAPTER 4

# BETWEEN-THE-SHEETS DRAMA

The first time I had sex I was seventeen years old. It was the summer of 1981 and I was about to go into my senior year of high school. The guy was someone I considered a boyfriend, but not a long-term boyfriend. He was just someone I was with until I got to the next situation.

We had sex in his basement. Back in the seventies and eighties, basements were big entertainment rooms. His parents were out. He pounded me hard, so hard that it left black-and-blue marks. I went to Belmar Beach the next day and all I could think about was, "I dumped it. I dumped my virtue on a man I didn't particularly care about."

Sex has gotten better over the years. My first few times, I didn't know what I was doing, so I didn't know what to ask for. It's gotten better because I've gotten more comfortable with myself. I used to love the touch of a new man, but now I prefer the familiarity of a steady lover. You can let yourself go. When you have an orgasm, you can cry because it just feels so good. And there is an emotional connection that takes it to the next level, beyond just the physical act and the pleasure. The ability to just lose yourself in the act of sex and not have to worry about being embarrassed or flawed is a beautiful thing.

## THREE'S A CROWD!

**My boyfriend told me for his thirtieth birthday he wants a threesome. Not happening. I don't share my man. How do I break the news?**

This is not an uncommon request from a guy. They love the idea of two women getting nasty on them. But this is not right for you, so you need to bring this right to your man: "I'm not sharing you today, tomorrow, or ever." Be firm and tell him to pick something else that doesn't involve a third party. There are a lot of fun, sexy things you can do as a duo. Pick up some toys, watch some raunchy DVDs, practice every position in the *Kama Sutra*. Get creative and he won't be disappointed!

**How much sex is too much? My new boyfriend is horny 24/7. The other night we did it like six times and I didn't get any sleep!**

Your relationship is brand-new. You're sexy. You're juicy. You're like a new toy that's fun to play with. Take this as a compliment and understand the sex will slow down at some point. Even the horniest man on the planet cuts back once he's married a few years. Doctors tell us that men have stronger libidos than women, and I do believe it. Take it from a woman who's been married to a horn dog for fifteen years, BE FLATTERED. Your man loves your body and finds you irresistible. Is that so bad? Open your legs and find a reason to rejoice.

The other thing to think about is your own feelings toward sex. Hormonally speaking, is your libido running low? If so, talk to your gyn. Sometimes a hormonal imbalance or even certain medications you are taking can dampen your drive.

## HOT TOPIC
### Kick-Starting Your Sex Drive

It happens to all of us at one time or another. You're tired. You're overworked. You're a new mom. For whatever reason, sex is the last thing on your mind. Men take a Viagra or read *Playboy* and they're good to go. But, girl, your plumbing is a little more complicated. After childbirth, stuff down there stretches out, dries up, and can even hurt. And come menopause, there's less estrogen circulating in your body, making your libido take a nosedive. So what's a woman to do? Glad you asked!

- **Talk to your doc.** She may do a blood test to check your thyroid function and iron. Both can affect sex drive. She can also talk to you about treatment that can increase both desire and sensation.

- **Get in the mood.** Light some candles . . . dim the lights . . . put on Barry White. Sometimes just setting the scene can jump-start things.

- **Read a raunchy book.** *Fifty Shades . . . Lady Chatterley's Lover . . . Zane . . .* whatever floats your boat. Let your mind be stimulated and watch what happens down below!

- **Watch some titillating TV.** Have you checked out some of those late-night shows on cable? How about XXX on Demand? Don't be a prude . . . pop in *Debbie Does Dallas.* Why not pop some popcorn and watch it in the buff together?

. . . . . . . . . . . . . . . . . . . . . . . . . . . . . . . . . . . .

**I've never had an orgasm unless I've used a vibrator. I'm totally faking each time I have sex with my husband. Should I tell my husband?**

Let me tell you what I do. I go to my gyn once a year, fully clothed, and I have a simple sit-down in her office to talk about things. I've had the same gyn for twenty-two years. She happens to be older than me, because I want to hear what an old dog has to say. If something isn't working for you, speak up. Gynos are great people. You can tell them anything, and they won't squirm. They've heard it and seen it all. Explain that you are having trouble climaxing with your husband. Maybe there is a good physical reason why, i.e., the position you're using (for example, missionary) isn't the right one based on your anatomy. Your gyn knows you inside and out and can offer some practical solutions.

As for a vibrator working wonders, this is good news. Introduce your man to your vibe. All men want to do is get us off—they don't particularly care how. Teach him how to please your lady bits and you won't be sorry. Give him instructions (don't criticize!) and moan and groan approvingly when he hits the right buttons. So do your research and give it a few months. I wouldn't tell your man till after that point. I'm sure by then you'll have figured out a way for him to make you happy.

**I have three kids and a full-time job and all I want to do is sleep. My husband keeps complaining that we don't have sex anymore. I'm just too exhausted!**

Of course you are, and I know you need a good night's sleep. But you have to carve out time for your man. I am older than my husband by seven years, and I have the same concerns as you: a kid and a full-time job that wipe me out physically and emotionally. There are plenty of times I am not in the mood, but I'll tell you what: I try to put all the business and school stuff out of my mind for twenty little minutes and show my man some attention. Sex has to be a priority in your life, or trust me, the marriage will suffer. It isn't just about pleasing your spouse, it's about connecting and staying intimate. Talk to your husband about helping you out with the kids. Offer him some trade-offs. Like, "If you get the kids bathed and into bed, I'll meet you in bed for a little fun . . . " Sex is also a great stress buster, not to mention a "cardio" exercise. It releases endorphins, those "feel good" chemicals that put a smile on your face. Isn't that worth making some time for?

**In college, I experimented with girls and now I am twenty-three and thinking about it again. There's this really cute girl at my gym who flirts with me. My boyfriend and I have been together for a year. Should I tell him I'm bi? What if he freaks?**

After a year of being with your boyfriend, you're just telling him you are bi? Why didn't you share this with him sooner—like when you decided you wanted to be in a serious relationship? Yeah, he's going to freak because you have been hiding a big part of who you are from him. If you are scoping out other girls, then the relationship is already going south. Flirting with a girl in the gym is no different from a straight girl flirting with a guy. It's off-limits. It's wrong. It's called cheating with your mind, and sounds to me like you are about to cheat with your body. So then I think you owe it to your boyfriend to be honest: "This isn't working for me and this is why: I'm bisexual."

He may not *completely* flip out. He may say, "I just hit the jackpot! Bring her home. Let's try her out." Most guys are psyched to have a threesome, but this is not a road you want to be going down. Your letter—and frankly your youth—tells me that you need to be single and free to experiment. Date guys. Date girls. Allow yourself to really figure out what and who you want.

## HOT TOPIC
### Breaking Up Is Not So Hard to Do

For whatever reason, you've decided it's over and you're dumping him. How do you let him down easy?

- **Be gentle.** Chances are he didn't see this one coming. Be as kind as you can, and don't make this all about what he did wrong or why you don't want him anymore. It takes two to tango, and you're both to blame for the relationship coming to an end.

- **Keep your cool.** No yelling, sobbing, hyperventilating, etc. I know what you're saying is difficult, but the more you keep your wits about you, the easier it will be.

- **Find the right time/place.** In public at a sushi bar or seated behind home plate at a Yankees game . . . probably not the ideal setting. Wait till you're alone, somewhere quiet, where you can talk without interruption or distraction.

- **Expect him to be hurt.** Or pissed. Or maybe even relieved. You never know how a guy is going to react to being a dumpee, so expect the unexpected.

- **Keep it between you.** Don't tell his mom, your roommate, your bowling league that you're breaking up with him before you do the deed. He should be the first person to hear the news.

- **Don't publicize it.** It's just not nice to change your Facebook status or broadcast your split on Twitter. Allow some time for it to sink in before you share the fact that you're on the market again.

. . . . . . . . . . . . . . . . . . . . . . . . . . . . . . . . . . . .

## I caught my husband watching porn on his computer one night. It totally freaked me out. What should I do?

Loosen up! Porn is not an OMG moment. I can tell you this: I like a little porn from time to time. I think it's hot. Maybe it makes your hubby feel the same way, and it puts him in the mood? "One night" is no biggie. If he's addicted and spending hours watching sex on-screen (instead of working or spending time with you), then that's a whole other story. Or if the porn was weird and not your garden variety (i.e., involving two men or underage girls/boys or violence). In my opinion, ya gotta ask him what he's watching—and not in a threatening, accusatory manner. Say something like "Honey, I noticed something interesting on your computer. Can you show me?" If he freaks out or tries to deny or hide it, then I would say you have a right to be a little concerned. But if he gladly shows you, then watch with an open mind. You might actually enjoy it.

**I like to be on top, but I'm heavy—like 250 pounds. My boyfriend says I smother him when we have sex. Missionary doesn't do it for me. Help!**

I'm a big girl, too, and I can tell you this: Not every position works for us. Have you tried propping things up with a firm pillow? Doggie style? You have to be willing to get adventurous and find ways that work for both of you. If none of the above solves your problem, then I'm going to say something you may not want to hear: Lose some weight. Sometimes a girl's gotta do what a girl's gotta do to make her life—and her sex—better.

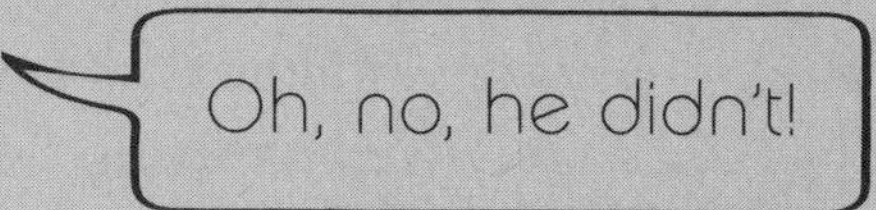


**My husband asked me if I would dress up as a maid, feather duster and everything, and have role-play sex with him for his birthday. I think it's kind of weird, do you?**

Dressing up as a maid is better than being asked to have a threesome like the previous letter! It's totally reasonable and, frankly, fun. Go on and channel *Downton Abbey* as you get down and dirty! Tie on an apron and talk with an accent. Serve him tea and crumpets in the buff. Experts say that fantasy role-play can add excitement to an otherwise mundane sex life. As children, we role-play as princesses or cowboys and Indians without a second thought. I say there's nothing wrong with indulging your man with a little dress-up drama. If it turns him on, why not? I wouldn't throw out any Halloween costumes if I were you . . .

**This guy I just started dating is unnaturally endowed down there, if you get my drift. After we slept together for the first time, it hurt like hell and I was walking funny the next day. What do I do?**

I find nothing wrong with dropping a guy if his plumbing is not suitable to your plumbing, shall we say. When I was single, I was certainly picky about penises. If you were not circumcised, I would drop you like a bad habit right away. If you were too big or too small, *hasta la vista,* baby. You might say this is very superficial of me. But I don't care how great your job is, how much money you make, or how great our conversation over dinner. If the parts don't fit together, then there is no need to continue the relationship.

So I say bail. I'm sorry, but sex is a very important part of a relationship. If it's going to be unpleasant, then you're doomed from the start. When the penis is not right, nothing will be right in the long haul. You're not going to stick me with that monster every night, I'm sorry.

**My mom walked in on me having sex with a guy. I'm over twenty-one, but I still live at home. She hasn't mentioned it. Should I?**

Do not mention it to your mother! What I would do, even in this bad economy, is get your butt looking for a place of your own. This is a warning shot, young lady. This is not just about your mother walking in on you banging some guy. This is about your mother being all up in your business. When you live in your parents' home, you have to live by their rules. It's time to move out so there are no other awkward, uncomfortable moments like this. You're a big girl. Get a roommate if you have to (or two!) but get moving out.

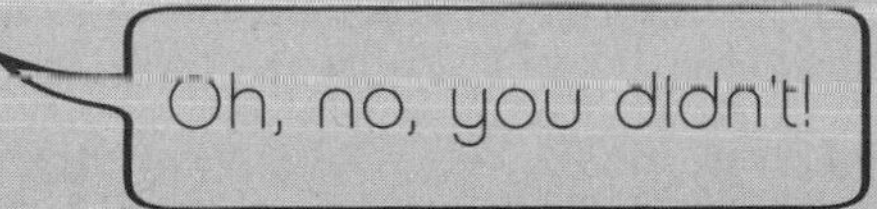


**A few weeks ago, I gave this guy I was dating a blow job and I accidentally clenched my teeth, and well, he's scared now to let me do it again. What should I do?**

Oh, honey. If he's that skittish, he hasn't had a lot of BJs before. This is a common faux pas that women make, and it's not that big a deal as long as your recovery is FABULOUS! Don't discuss it any further—no apologies. Just roll your lips over your teeth and continue. Guys love blow jobs, even bad ones. He'll get over it. Just be more careful next time!

**I feel like I'm having Cirque du Soleil sex. My boyfriend likes to try all these crazy positions in bed. Last night I fell off the bed and smacked my head. Help!**

I've read your letter three times and the only thing I can find that's wrong with this situation is that you smacked your head. So move your night table! Put some pillows around the floor to break your fall. Cirque du Soleil sex sounds great to me. Crazy positions in bed are natural requests from guys, and usually loved by women. Is that what's really worrying you? Not the threat of a concussion, but that this guy's sexual escapades are not what you are used to? Let loose and have fun. I hear from way too many women who are nervous and insecure about their sexuality. I think this guy could teach you a thing or two, and not just about sex. I think he could help you let go of your inhibitions. Enjoy!

**I told my boyfriend once to spank me in bed and now he thinks it's fun and gets turned on by it. My ass is black-and-blue. How do I get him to stop what I started?**

Anything we say to guys, they take it to the twentieth level. All the time. Now, what you can do is talk to your boyfriend outside of a sexual situation and gently tell him you're not loving the spankings. Suggest he engage in a little love tap instead—something softer and gentler that doesn't leave you bruised. Since it was your suggestion, I assume you don't want him to stop, just to ease up a bit. Don't make this a part of every single love session. Mix it up a bit! Talk to your man, I'm sure he'll understand.

**My husband sucks in bed. I kind of knew this before we got married, but I thought he'd get better with practice. I gave him a great sex how-to DVD for his birthday (hint, hint!), but he never watched it. Am I destined for a marriage of bad sex?**

Uh, yeah . . . unless you show and tell. Men love to work our bodies like a Stradivarius violin. They want to see us howl with delight and squeal with orgasms. Your man will be open to your suggestions if you just reintroduce him to your body and how you like it to be touched. As for the DVD, frankly, if I were him, I would have been insulted! Talk to your husband. This conversation is just as important as the monthly grocery bill. The good news is that any man can learn to be a better lover . . . with a little coaching.

Oh, no, you didn't!

**About a week ago, I peed during sex. We were going pretty hot and heavy and it just happened. I'm worried that the guy I was with will never want to sleep with me again. What should I do?**

Mention it to your man. Mention it in a tongue-in-cheek, LOL kind of way: "The sex was so good, baby. It was so hot and heavy, and I had so many orgasms, that I got a little carried away and may have wet the sheets a little . . ." Let me let you in on a little secret: Guys don't care what we do during sex. We can cry. We can swear like a truck driver. We can pee on them. All they care about is getting off. I don't want you to continue to worry or feel self-conscious about this. Sex is a time to let your body go. Who knows—maybe you had a "female ejaculation." They exist, you know! If he even noticed at all, I think he'll get over this real quick. He will think he is God's gift to women. If it really bothers you, then do some

Kegel exercises to strengthen your bladder (your gyn can tell you how) and make a trip to the little girls' room before you get down to business.

**I dozed off during sex with my husband. It wasn't on purpose; I was just tired. The strange thing is, he didn't even notice. What should I do?**

Don't tell him. If he didn't notice, don't say a word. Hopefully, you didn't snore and he was otherwise occupied! Falling asleep during sex is highly insulting. You don't want to make it a habit. Next time, have a hit of Red Bull so it doesn't happen again!

**My boyfriend asked me what my number was. I didn't want to tell him because I was kind of a slut in high school and college and I'm afraid it will scare him off. I lost count around thirty-seven. Should I lie?**

What does your number matter to who you are today? You're a better—and hopefully more discriminating—person than you were in high school and college. Most of us are better people today than we were back then. I don't believe in sharing numbers. If he insists you spill, I would tell a little white lie. There is a double standard here. A high number for a guy signals expertise. For a woman, it means she's loose. So here's what you do: Divide your number by two and subtract three. That's my formula. Besides that, have a conversation that explains the number: "You know, baby, I don't keep count of how many people I've had sex with because the only person that matters to me is you . . ." Don't get in an argument with him over this. Change the topic if you can and put the past behind you.

**I was having sex with this guy and he asked me if my boobs were real or fake. I kinda lied. They're fake. But c'mon, who is born with triple D's? Do I fess up or let him think I'm a goddess?**

I say what he doesn't know won't hurt him. Why confess truth to just "a guy you're having sex with." To me, that means he's a hookup. He barely needs to know the truth about your real name. Until he's more to you than a plaything, you don't owe him an explanation. But . . . there is going to come a time in your life when you meet a guy whom you really care about—the one who's a keeper. With this man, you want to be honest. You want to tell him about any plastic surgery you have had, because one day, when you're married for fifteen years and your boobs suddenly deflate (I know what I am talking about here!), he's going to sure-as-hell figure it out. But until things are serious, your boobs are nobody's business but your own.

**I got drunk and I think I screwed my shore-house roommate. I'm not sure because it's all a blur. He hasn't mentioned it. What should I do?**

You *think*? As in, maybe you did or maybe you didn't? If he hasn't made any mention, chances are it's all hazy to him as well. So in my opinion, you should keep your mouth shut and your legs closed around him. Pretend it never happened (because it may not have!). As for going forward, please be careful of how much you drink. I know how easy it is to party too hard and lose control, but think of the repercussions now when you're sober. You don't want to get an STD or knocked up because you were too bombed to think clearly and use a condom.

**My boyfriend wants me to have sex in a public place, i.e., bathrooms, the lawn in Central Park, taxis. He says it turns him on. I've done it a couple of times, but I feel like a perv. What should I do?**

Given this guy's preference for screwing in public view, it's probably safer for you to have sex with him on the Great Lawn in Central Park than in his apartment. You never know: He may be taping you to post on YouTube later! But personally . . . I love risky sex. It livens the party. It mixes things up. It takes things out of the bedroom and spices up your love life. If your boyfriend wants to have sex with you in public places, open your mind and explore. Can I tell you a little story? About five years ago, my hubby and I came home from being out late and we were in the mood. We weren't sure if our son or the babysitter was awake, so we did it on a concrete bench on the front lawn behind some bushes. All of a sudden, right in the middle of him slaying me like a dragon, the sprinklers came on. We were soaked, but we had a great laugh out of it and appreciated our little "adventure" in the great outdoors. Loosen up, and maybe make an adventure or two of your own.

## WENDY'S FINAL WORD

### How to Have Great Sex Sans the Drama

The key to great lovemaking in my book is the three C's: connection, communication, and coitus—the actual act of getting it on has to be worth remembering! Like most things in life, the more you practice, the better it gets . . .

- **He will want it more than you.** Always. Guys have a greater sexual appetite. Once you understand this, you can make peace with it. Know that his penis is calling the shots and act accordingly.

- **Know your body.** Sit on a mirror. Know your body parts. Masturbate. Get to know what makes you feel good. I'm a liberated woman, and if I'm making you blush, I apologize. But there is no way a man is ever going to please you if you don't know how to please yourself.

Talk to your gyn and get yourself sexually educated.

- **Sex never goes out of style.** Even if, like me, you've been with your man for a long time, sex should still be an important part of your relationship. But couples tend to let it slide: A majority of men (54 percent) and nearly as many women (42 percent) said they were unhappy with the frequency of sex, according to the report in the *Journal of Sex and Marital Therapy*. I say older doesn't have to mean colder.

- **Keep it fresh.** Try new things and that includes new places: the side of the road, the back of the restaurant after you've had your meal, your backyard behind the bushes (my personal fave). Try role-play, talking dirty, a XXX movie marathon now and then. The point is to think outside the box and the bedroom.

# CHAPTER 5

# MAMA DRAMA

If you've got a mother—or you are a mother—you've known your share of mama drama. I can say with one hundred percent certainty that if my mother were my age, we would not be friends. I treasure her—but we are such different people. She freaked out when I was posing nude for PeTA. She hates that we will let our son watch *South Park* and that we swear in front of him. Let's just say Mommy and I don't always see eye to eye . . .

While I was growing up, my mom was a beautiful, brilliant woman, and very physically fit. I wasn't; I was Fat Wendy who could not get above a C in most classes to save her own life. But we started to connect as soon as I found myself and solidified my success. She loves that lady I now am, and I have to say, I appreciate her more now that I am a mother as well. We've made our peace. And when I stack her up against everyone else's mom, no one is as good. She's smart. (She has a double master's!) She's stylish. She's got a great sense of humor. She knows how to make lemonade out of lemons.

When I first had Kevin, I was not able to breast-feed. He was ravenous and my breasts hurt. I was not good at expressing the milk. I had been on bed rest for nine months, and I was a career girl and just wanted to go back to work and lose the baby weight—all 103 pounds of it!

One day, when Kevin was just a couple of weeks old, I collapsed in our bedroom. That's where my mom found me, hiding from the world. I was crying and very upset that I had no one to talk to. I thought that breast-feeding was supposed to be as natural as walking. But not for me. Not by a long shot. I felt like I was failing the whole mother thing. I was letting my son down, and he was barely a month old!

My mom sat down on the floor with me and hugged me—which was quite a feat. I'm gigantic compared to her. My mom is a tiny lady of five feet two inches; I'm this five-eleven giant, who weighed 290 pounds at the time.

"What's the matter?" she asked softly, pushing my hair to one side and letting me bury my tearful face in her shoulder. "Mommy, I can't do it," I sobbed. "I want to, but I can't."

My mom nodded. "Wendy, don't you worry." Then she called downstairs to my dad: "Tom! Bring the car around! We're going to the grocery store."

There, she stocked up on four months of Carnation Good Start for me to feed the baby. She told me that she did not breast-feed me or my siblings, and it was okay if I couldn't. Good Start was good enough for us and it would be good enough for Kevin.

My mom is a naturally bossy woman who always expected greatness from me—so this moment of understanding and tenderness floored me. It was the beginning of a wonderfully close—yet flawed—mother/daughter relationship. I am grateful that my mom was there for me and shared with me. In many ways, she gave me permission that day to be a not-so-perfect mom. Thirteen years later, I can tell you I am a damn good one. But perfect? Nah!

**We're newly married, and I swear, my mother-in-law hates me. She is always criticizing me. She doesn't like the way I cook, how I dress, etc. How do I tell her to butt out of my life?**

Sounds like your mommy-in-law dearest is threatened by your new role in her baby boy's life. Unfortunately, when you marry the guy, you also marry his family. Have your tried making nice-nice? Taking her to lunch? Buying her a new car (kidding!). I'm sure you have, and you've reached the end of your rope because nothing you do or say is good enough. Time to get your hubby on your side. He may not want to talk back to his mama, but this is not negotiable. You are not going to submit to being bashed by this bitch in mom's clothing. And as far as the way you cook, if she doesn't like it, she doesn't have to eat it. How you dress? Who made her a *Project Runway* judge? Eventually, she'll either back off (for fear of losing her darling son further) or die. Either way, don't let it get to you. You be the person you are, because that's the woman your husband fell in love with.

**This divorced mother in my kid's class dumps her son on me for playdates, then goes out on dates and doesn't come back until nine o'clock to pick him up. I'm not a babysitter, and I feel used and abused.**

When she goes out on a date and doesn't show up until 9 P.M., that's not her fault. That's your fault for tolerating it. I would have been texting and calling her until she got her ass back home, date or no date. You are going to call her on the carpet for what she's done wrong. And then you are going to grow a backbone and tell her if she wants a sitter recommendation, you're happy to get her some. It just ain't gonna be you! Choose your words carefully and refrain from using the B-word. This is the mother of a kid in your son's class. If things don't work out, it could get ugly for your child. Be firm but friendly: "I did you a favor this time, but I'm not comfortable with this happening again."

**My dad recently passed away and my mom is depressed and miserable. I beg her to go out to a widows' support group or grief counseling, but she refuses. She says it won't help because it won't bring him back. What can I do to help her?**

I know what you're saying, because my parents are old school, too. They don't like people knowing their business or "talking" about their problems. What you can do to help your mother is bring her all the information from the support groups. You can lead her to the water, but you can't make her drink. I know you want to help, but it's her choice to live this way. You can explain to her that her depression upsets and worries you, and you wish she would try, just try, reaching out to other people who are familiar with her situation. Be patient—this is relatively new to her, and the grief is probably overwhelming. Be a good listener. Offer her whatever she needs, even if it's just your shoulder to cry on for now.

**My mother-in-law is friends with my husband's ex-wife. They were married for two years and they've been divorced for five. So why are his mother and his ex talking on the phone and going out to lunch? It's bugging the crap out of me. What should I do?**

Take a deep breath and remember this: You are the one he is with now—not the evil ex. I don't like this situation any more than you do, but obviously your mother-in-law forged a bond with her son's former spouse. I don't blame any of the women involved in this triangle; I blame your hubby. He needs to insist in no uncertain terms that his mother discontinue her "intimate" relationship with his ex. She can stay in touch with her casually without rubbing it in your face. If he doesn't defend your honor here, he's muddying the waters for you and your mother-in-law and preventing you two from ever having a decent relationship. Make him understand how inappropriate and plain annoying this is for you. If he doesn't want a second ex, he'll intervene.

**I feel like all I do is run around and take my three kids to school, soccer, swim team, and gymnastics. I have no life. Help!**

I was just having this conversation the other day with one of my mom friends. I'm always crazy running around with my son, and I have just one kid. My friend has three like you, and I swear, I don't know how she finds time to pee, much less eat. Welcome to the world of motherhood—having no life comes with the job title. But it doesn't *always* have to be this way. Organization and delegation are key. Do you have any help? Can you and your husband plan some sort of schedule? Can he pitch in and give you a break? Can you hire a sitter or a mother's helper to ease the load?

I promise you, one day you will have a life again. Kids grow up fast. Right now you have to grab every bit of in-between time you can find between your kids' social and school calendars and make the most of it for yourself. For me, it means chilling out and relaxing. I need to watch a *Brideszilla* marathon or pull out all of my magazines, my *Life & Style,* my *Star,* my *Enquirer,* my *WWD.* I need to polish my nails or soak in a bubble bath. It takes no more than twenty minutes and you will feel human again. Hang in there!

**My twenty-one and twenty-three-year-old daughters have keys to my house, but I don't have keys to theirs. I think it's unfair and unsafe. What do you think?**

I'll be honest with you: When I was their age (and even now at almost fifty years old), I didn't want my parents to have a key to my house. My parents have chosen to give me keys to their homes in case of emergencies, but I would never just "pop in" on them. The issue here is respect: respecting your daughters' privacy and independence. They've got their own lives now, and you've got yours. What I would say to you? Here ya go: Change your lock. It's time for some new rules. You don't need a key to your girls' apartments, but they also don't need a key to yours. If you're going out for a while and need them to check in on the dog or water the plants, you can keep a spare. But no more *"mi casa, su casa." Comprende?*

Oh, no, he didn't!

**My husband says that I need to dress more mommish now that I've had a baby. I'm sorry but I like my clothes a little bit sexy and a little bit tight. Is there anything wrong with that?**

Girl, you sound like me. I was willing to become a mom, but not willing to give up my Wendy-licious style. I'm a Jersey girl. I like all things cheetah and leopard print. I love hairspray. I love sexy. Sorry. I do. There is nothing wrong with your attitude. Your husband needs to get over this whole "you're a mom now" thing and encourage you to dress any way that makes you feel beautiful and confident. Mamas today are HAWT and he's lucky to have a woman who turns heads when she walks down the street. You go!

**I don't believe in spanking, but my mother-in-law obviously does. She was babysitting my six-year-old son last night and he told me, "I was really bad and Gram hit my tushy." I'm really pissed and what should I do?**

Bring it right to your mother-in-law. I do not believe in grandparents parenting our children, and it was not her job to discipline your son. I grew up with spankings, and I don't believe I am more warped than anyone else. However, no one is to lay hand to behind except for mom and dad. Grandparents are not there to spank. Aunts, uncles, nephews, schoolteachers, nobody! You better not spank my kid, you hear me? You and your husband need to talk about how you believe his parent has overstepped her boundaries. And please, don't make your son feel like a double agent for telling on his grams. Assure him it was a good thing, and do your best to make sure it doesn't happen again.

**Wendy, we're new in town, and moms in my kid's kindergarten are snubbing me. I've asked for lunch or coffee or tried to arrange a playdate, but everyone says, "I'm sorry." I feel like**

## this is high school and the popular girls won't let me in the clique.

My first reaction is to say, "Screw 'em" and be on your merry way. But this isn't just about you—it's about your child's future. So you push your way into this clique and you don't take no for an answer. This is your Meryl Streep moment. You need to act the part to get into the circle. Volunteer for lice checks. Solicit auction prizes. Chair the bake sale. You know what I'm talking about: Take on the tasks that no one else wants so they think you're a selfless giver. Maybe these women will never accept you, but for kindergarten, you're gonna make them tolerate you. I know that sucking up sucks, but consider this an intelligence-gathering exercise. Learn the lay of the land; the good teachers and the bad ones; which kids eat glue and which moms give really good birthday gifts. Dig, dig, dig, but don't let them know you're doing it. Watch a few episodes of *Homeland* and you'll be good to go.

## WENDY'S FINAL WORD

### Tips to Minimize Mama Drama

- **Understand, at some point** (usually when you're twenty-one and an adult living on your own) **your mother is no longer the matriarch of the family.** She is just another participant whom you respect, but she is no longer the leader who gets to be the boss of you. She may not understand this, but you do. And you live your life accordingly.

- **Don't compare yourself to other mothers.** I have a very good friend whose children speak Chinese; my kid needs a tutor to speak plain English! For many years I thought I was an inadequate mother because I wasn't pushing my kid to take violin, join the math team, and run track. I thought I wasn't doing the best for him. Then I realized a lot of women treat motherhood as a competitive sport. It isn't about what the child likes or needs; it's about bragging rights. I will never master Mandarin and neither will Little Kev—and I'm cool with that.

- **Take care of yourself.** You spend so much time nurturing everyone in your family that you never make any time for yourself. Honey, that is a one-way ticket to misery and a nervous breakdown. I beg you, be good to yourself. Make time for doctor and dentist appointments; get your roots dyed and your nails done. You are a person, too, and don't you ever forget it.

- **Don't be a martyr.** By this, I mean if you need help, ask for it. Ask your husband, your neighbor, your mom, your sis—anyone who can lend a hand when you feel like you're going under. There are days I will turn to Big Kevin and say, "You have got to handle this for me." And he does. And I feel better. I feel like a huge burden is off my shoulders. You don't have to be a Superwoman all the time.

- **Change the rules.** This is your right as a mother. If something isn't working for you, your child, your family as a whole, then change it. There is nothing set in stone, and the most together moms I know are also the most flexible. They realize that shit happens, and you have to think on your feet and react. They don't get swept up in drama, because they know how to divert it with a little ingenuity and a quick rewrite.

. . . . . . . . . . . . . . . . . . . . . . . . . . . . . . . . . . .

## CHAPTER 6

# FAMILY DRAMA

Unless you are a recluse living alone on a desert island, the people you call your relatives will drive you nuts at some point in your life. That's what families do. But I'll tell you something: I don't let these things get to me. I'm just so appreciative in this post-9/11, post-Katrina, post–Hurricane Sandy, post-Newtown shooting world that I have these people in my life. I let the stupid stuff roll off my back. This might sound morbid to you, but I am keenly aware that at any given moment, any one of my family members could be gone. Unfortunately, that's the crazy world we live in. So I made up my mind: I'm not going to spend time fighting with them. I'm not going to hold a grudge or make a mountain out of a molehill. Life is short, my friends. Way too short.

**My sister-in-law is a know-it-all bitch. She's always telling me I'm overprotective and I'm screwing up my kids. How do I tell her to "back off!" My kids. My rules.**

This woman sounds like a handful! But here's the thing: As long as you are married to your husband, she's gonna be a part of your family and your kids' auntie. She'll be at holiday get-togethers and weddings and funerals, so you can't just dismiss her. In my opinion, you should pull in your husband and explain what's going on. Get him on your team and have him talk to her. She needs to understand that when she criticizes you, she is also slamming him because you make parenting decisions together. He needs to tell her to back off, and as her bro, he'll know exactly the way to do that. As for her nasty comments, it sounds like you are paying them no mind. Good girl! Don't react or take the bait. Live your life the way you want and don't let her bully you.

**My fiancé just told me that his dad once served time for robbery. He says it's no biggie. It was when he was young. But I'm a little freaked to be marrying into a family of ex-cons.**

Wow, what a bomb your fiancé dropped on you! Take a deep breath: Last time I checked, armed robbery was not one of those traits that gets passed down in families, generation to generation. If his dad's out, he's paid his debt. It was, as your fiancé said, when he was younger. Water under the bridge. If your fiancé's a good *thang,* and this is your only complaint, I don't think you have anything to worry about. I commend him for being honest with you. Now you do the right thing and forget about it.

**My nineteen-year-old little brother has a drinking problem and my parents refuse to see it. I'm twenty-one, and we both live at home, so I see him come in every night wasted. They say he's just a "normal teenager," but I'm worried that he's going to hurt himself or someone else. What should I do?**

I must say, as the big sister, you have a lot on your shoulders right now. This is a situation that needs to be handled very delicately or your family could fall apart and everyone will blame you for butting in. Your parents are probably in denial. No one wants to hear that a child is a hot mess. Sounds like your bro can do no wrong in their eyes. I would suggest the next time he stumbles through the door drunk, you wake them up and let them see for themselves how serious this situation is becoming. Have you also simply tried to talk to your brother, sibling to sibling, young person to young person, and let him know that you know the score? If you haven't—for fear of confrontation—then do your research. Have your Web sites, your publications, your AA meeting schedules. Make it easy for him to get help if he is ready to do so. Tell him how you feel: You love him, you care about him, and you don't want to see him make mistakes that could impact the rest of his life and the lives of the people around him.

I know you're worried, but you cannot stop a person who is addicted. Trust me, I know. It's no secret that there was a time in my life when I was heavily involved in illegal substances. My drug of choice was cocaine. Nobody could tell me anything. Thankfully, I ended up cleaning myself up after realizing I was at a dead end, and I was hurting everyone around me. But I can't promise you that your brother will be ready to do the same. Be supportive, but also know this isn't your issue to fix. You can only do so much. Your parents have to take some responsibility, and he has to want to change.

## HOT TOPIC
### Fixing Family Feuds

It's a fact . . . families fight. Many times it's over something silly or material, like money or who is Mom's favorite. Tired of the tiffs? Try these tips.

- **Don't hold a grudge.** Seriously, get over it. No matter what was done or said, is it worth it to not speak to your brother for two years?
- **Be the bigger person.** Step up and mend the rift, even if no one else is willing to. If you wait for someone else to make the first move, you might be waiting forever.
- **Be open-minded.** There are two sides to every story, so don't be quick to side with one family member over another.
- **Be patient.** Not every disagreement can be resolved overnight. Sometimes feelings are hurt and nerves are raw. Allow matters to cool down before stepping in.

**I'm twenty-four years old and my parents are getting divorced. I know I'm not a kid and I shouldn't freak out, but I am.**

That's a perfectly natural reaction, honey bun. I'm a grown woman, damn near fifty myself, and I would freak out if my parents split. Why? Because when your family foundation is suddenly torn apart, it's very hard to deal—no matter how many years you've got under your belt. I get it. However, you know these two people, and you know that their great love produced you. Talk to each of your parents separately. Try to find out as much information as you can so you can understand and accept the situation better. For all you know, your mom and dad are fine with divorcing each other and will remain friends. If you have siblings, talk to them. Know that although your folks' relationship is changing, your relationship with each of them isn't. They still love you and you still love them.

**My eighty-five-year-old grandmother has dementia and my mother wants to move her in with her and my dad. I feel this will be a huge burden on my parents, and she'd be better off in a**

**nursing home. But Mom says no way, that's not happening. Should I mind my own business?**

I feel for you, I truly do. Your mom is upset and worried and feels a sense of obligation here—but she's not thinking clearly. Caring for someone with dementia is difficult, stressful, and all-consuming. If she allows your grandmother to move in, her life—and her marriage to your dad—will never be the same. It's going to be a huge drain on both of them. Has she thought of every option? Is there a living situation that is near to her home so she could visit your grandma every day? What about in-home nursing care so the burden is not always on her? Perhaps you could do a little digging and present some alternatives to her? Another thing you can tell her is that people with dementia often benefit from being in assisted living. A structured routine can minimize your grandmother's fears and she'll have constant companionship. I know this is a tough decision for all of you; but you do have choices. I suggest you talk to a support group for caregivers such as the Alzheimer's Association (www.alz.org). It will help a great deal to know you're not alone.

**My husband bought a dog for Christmas for the kids without asking**

**me. He pees all over the place and chews the furniture, and I'm the only one who walks it. If I wanted another "baby" to take care of, I would have one.**

I hate to sound harsh, but how dare your husband make such a major decision without asking you! Your household is made up of equal parts—50 percent your opinion and 50 percent his. He had no right to do this without consulting you. So here's what you should do: Return the dog. Sell it back to the place where he bought it, or find it a good home with a friend or neighbor who wants a pet. Don't even ask your husband. This will make him very upset, but he will also understand that "This household is not just about your decisions. You should have come to me to begin with." Then you are going to go to your kids and tell them (you ready for this one?) "the dog ran away." Yup. Because you don't want them to hate you and think you're Scrooge for sending Fido back.

All the things you are telling me are all the things that I've been through. It broke my heart, but I am still convinced I did the right thing. To this day, my household still does not have a dog. Ya know why? Because our son is into asking for a dog but not into all the responsibility. My husband would get the dog, but guess who'd be stuck scooping the poop on the corner?

Neither of them, that's for sure. So no more dog . . . case closed!

**My husband keeps saying how much he wants to start a family. I'm really into my job and I don't want to get pregnant now. I'm thirty-one and I feel like I have plenty of time to have a baby later. What should I do?**

I refuse, personally speaking, to give up control of my own body, and I would not advise another woman to give up control either. So if now is not the time, then you have the right to make that decision. But eventually you're going to have to get in the baby-making business. Like it or not, the clock is ticking. What you should do is use age thirty-five as your cutoff. Your start time is thirty-three, and I think that's a fair compromise for your hubby. Please understand that even if you do have a baby (or two or three), that doesn't mean your career and your life are over. I am a working mother, and I make it work. Things will be harder, for sure, but you shouldn't think that you can't have both, a family and a job. It's 2013; honey, we can have it all! Being a mom is the most fulfilling, most challenging, most amazing job a woman could ever have. Don't deprive yourself of this experience!

• • • • • • • •

## QUIZ: HOW YOU DOIN'? AM I READY TO BE A MOM?

You *think* you're ready to take on motherhood . . . but oh, baby, you have no idea what's involved! Answer the questions and check your score below.

1. A typical Saturday night for me is:
   a. Clubbing till dawn and drinking till I puke.
   b. Dinner out with friends.
   c. Snuggling on the couch with my man and a tub of popcorn.

2. Your ideal getaway would be:
   a. Backpacking through the Himalayas.
   b. Sun, sand, and surf.
   c. Disney World.

3. In five years' time, you see yourself:
   a. President of my own company . . . and keeping company with assorted hotties.
   b. Settled down in a job and with a great guy.
   c. Changing diapers and watching *Dora the Explorer.*

4. How would you describe your parents' relationship?
   a. Armageddon.

b. Solid as a rock.

c. All about me.

5. Who is your mom role model?

a. Snooki.

b. Michelle Obama.

c. Mother Teresa.

**If you have mostly A's:** Honey, diaper duty is the farthest thing from your mind these days! You need to sow your oats and get it all out of your system before you settle down.

**If you have mostly B's:** You possess a calm, controlled lifestyle and outlook that would support a munchkin or two. Mommyhood is definitely on your radar.

**If you have mostly C's:** Girl, you have babies on the brain! Is your partner as gung ho to have kids as you? If so . . . put down this book and get down to business!

• • • • • • • •

**My husband's best friend is a loser. He's lost his job and his apartment, and he's always borrowing money from us. Now he's asked my husband to cosign a loan for him. How do I get my husband to get rid of this deadbeat?**

I am cosigning with YOU on this. I don't like this dude draining your bank account. It has got to stop! I hope your hubby is not loaning more than you can afford. This is becoming detrimental to your financial future and your relationship. Is your husband even aware that cosigning a loan will affect the amount of money and credit you as a couple can have? Your man is generous and compassionate and loyal—all great qualities. But his friend is taking advantage of him. Sit down with your husband and tell him no. No more lending or loaning. His pal needs to stand on his own two feet and you need to stand united on this as a couple.

**My husband's ex-girlfriend showed up ten years later and told him she has a twelve-year-old daughter by him. Obviously, she wants something. What should I do?**

Yeah, what she wants is twelve years of back child support. Look, this is a bad situation all the way around. I would not hate on the ex-girlfriend. She's apparently carried this burden for ten years. She hasn't bothered him. She's tried to go it alone. She hasn't been the scum of the earth pounding on windows and doors and blowing up telephones and taking him to court. She is a better woman than I would be, because I would have contacted him right away and demanded DNA. I would have made him pay through the nose.

So that's where I want you to start, with a DNA test. Make sure the kid is really his. And if she is, then you should stand by your husband. I know that's a short statement and a long task. I don't know how much this woman wants financially or emotionally. Is she expecting you to welcome this little girl into your family fold? And how does your husband feel about it? Does he want to be her daddy, or simply write a check? Talk to him; don't judge.

**My sister broke up with her boyfriend three months ago. We bumped into each other at a party and he asked me out. He's really cute and sweet—but is he off-limits?**

You better believe it—and I am sure you already know that in your bones or you wouldn't be asking. So hands off, honey! This can only lead to major trouble between you and your sis, not to mention the rest of your family. In my opinion, if he screwed (literally and figuratively) one of you, than he is persona non grata. That goes for one-night stands, hookups, even drive-bys. There are plenty of other "cute and sweet" guys out there. Why are you considering one of your sister's castoffs? I also want you to think about this: Maybe he is asking you out to screw with her. Maybe he wants to make her jealous or angry as payback. Do you really want to play those games? I am telling you, nothing good can come of this. Tell him thanks but no thanks.

## WENDY'S FINAL WORD

### Tips for Avoiding Family Drama

- **Set boundaries.** When you allow your relatives to invade your privacy and get all up in your business, you're inviting unwanted opinions and trouble.

- **Keep calm.** Nobody knows how to push your buttons like your family members. Take a deep breath and try not to react. If they see they can't get a rise out of you, they'll get bored and move on.

- **Don't gossip.** Don't rat out your brother to your mom; don't bitch about your mother-in-law to your sister-in-law. Trust me . . . it'll get back to them. And then you've just gotten more people involved in your mess.

- **Be the bigger person.** Say you're sorry; make peace; extend an olive branch. The longer you let disagreements fester, the harder they are to fix.

- **Stay away from touchy subjects.** If you know your sis is sensitive about her weight, then don't bring it up at a family dinner. Understand that some topics are off the table—especially if everyone is gathered around it.

- **Family is family.** Blood is thicker than water. You're stuck with them, so you might as well make the best of it!

.................................

## CHAPTER 7

# KID DRAMA

My "Little Kev" is about to become a teenager this summer. He's turning thirteen. I'm not stressed out . . . that much. My husband and I have done the best we can up until this point. He's smart and polite. He's a nice-looking boy and all the girls love him. We have open, honest conversations with him. My only fear is that when he becomes a teen, those conversations will stop. He'll turn to his friends for advice and the outside world's opinion will matter more to him than mine.

We've been going out for lunch every single Saturday since he was born. No Double Value Meal; we go to a reasonably good restaurant with a linen tablecloth and sit across from each other and talk about life. He shares everything with me, from school to sports to girls to issues he's having with his guy friends. I listen to him very intently and he hears me out. I tell him that I will kill him if he has a baby before it's time. I tell him he owes me sixteen years of school, and I want a four-year college. I get a lot of "Aw, Mommy!" and eye rolling when I say these things, but he knows I mean business.

We have an amazing relationship. My son really does love and respect me. He respects me as his mother and also as someone who has lived long and hard enough to know right from wrong. He will tell me when he likes my outfit or doesn't. He will literally say, "Mommy, you look hot!" That's just the bee's knees. I love him. I just love him. No matter how crazy your kids drive you, no matter how much they worry you, you love them more than words can say.

**A few moms have called me to complain that my son is a bully. They say he punches and threatens other kids in his fourth-grade class at recess. I've asked him to stop, but he won't. What can I do?**

Mom, you're being bullied by your son, too. That's why you are writing me this letter and not doing what you know needs to be done. Bullying is serious—it causes not just physical but emotional damage. It starts now with a few blows in the school yard, but it can continue (if you ignore it) into the teen years, when cruel remarks can spread like wildfire via the Internet. You say you've asked him to stop and he hasn't. So now you need to take stronger action. A child who bullies other children needs help—this is not normal boy behavior, so don't fool yourself into thinking it. You should schedule a parent–teacher conference and find out what's going on and why. You may have to get the principal, assistant principal, or a school guidance counselor or psychologist involved. For whatever reason, your son feels the need to take his aggression out on his peers. Where is that anger coming from? Who is he targeting and why? Make it clear that you will not, I repeat NOT, tolerate this behavior—and go along with the punishment the school recommends. It's your responsibility as his mom to nip this in the bud.

**My teenage daughter is a klepto. I found a bunch of stuff with tags in her closet, and I know I didn't buy them. What should I do?**

Bring this drama right to your daughter. Tell her you saw her closet, tags hanging, and you want to know how she paid for these things. You suspect that your child is a thief—let's call a spade a spade and deal with it. Even after you talk to her, you still might need family counseling or a support group (www.kleptomaniacsanonymous.com) to see you through it. Kids steal for a lot of reasons, oftentimes because they want attention. Some do it for the thrill; others because they're trying to piss you off and it's a way of rebelling. I don't know the reason, but I do know this: Your child is old enough to understand that what she is doing is wrong, not to mention against the law. I would not go easy on her. March her back to the store and make her return the clothes and apologize. Hopefully the embarrassment will deter her from doing it again.

## HOT TOPIC
### How to Know When Your Kid Is Lying

We want to trust them, but God knows, they don't make it easy. Pinocchio's nose grew when he fibbed. If only we were that lucky!

- **Look him/her in the eye.** If returning your gaze is tough, he's probably not being honest.

- **Watch body language.** Does he squirm in his seat? Is she twirling her hair? Bingo—it's probably a whopper!

- **Back him into a corner.** If your kid is avoiding you like the plague, it's for a good reason—he doesn't want to tell you something. Sit him down and confront him.

- **Listen for long silences.** If your kid has to hem and haw and hesitate while telling you a story, she's probably making it up as she goes along.

- **Beware of "best behavior."** If your kid did something wrong and doesn't want to fess up to it, he or she may try to overcompensate. Did she make her bed this A.M.? Do her homework without being nagged? Uh-oh . . .

. . . . . . . . . . . . . . . . . . . . . . . . . . . . . . . . . . . . . . .

**I worry about our toddler. He's almost three years old and doesn't talk a lot. He has trouble focusing, and I think there is something wrong. My husband says there's nothing wrong and to stop making a big deal out of it. He won't let me take him to the doctor.**

Don't ask his permission. Deception is not right, but sometimes it is very, very necessary. In this case, I want you to follow your gut. You know that your son's behavior is not normal. He might have mild autism or a learning disability, and he needs to be assessed by a professional. Many things are treatable with early intervention. But if you don't do something now, you won't be able to give your son the quality of life he deserves. I suspect your spouse doesn't want to hear anything is wrong—it hurts or scares him. Make the appointment. Take your toddler to an expert. Then fill your hubby in on what you find out and involve him in the rest of the process. It will be easier to talk about and deal with once you know what is or isn't wrong.

**My ten-year-old hates his teacher. He says she's mean and always accusing him of doing stuff. He claims it's because he's black and she's white. If this is the case, I'm going to kick her ass. What should I do?**

The manipulation of the black/white thing is as old as dirt. Sometimes it's true and sometimes it's not. Children know how to press our buttons as parents, particularly when we are minority parents. As a black mother myself, I know it would be too easy for Little Kev to get off the school bus and claim that a teacher doesn't like him because he's black. But I am too intelligent and too well versed in race relationships to let everything deteriorate into something as simplistic as prejudice. This requires further investigation on your part. You've got to speak to your school officials, including this teacher, and find out if these accusations have any weight. Don't go kicking anyone's ass off the bat—that's not going to teach your son about being tolerant.

**My fifteen-year-old daughter went to a party and came home wasted. I'm so pissed. I grounded her ass, but how do I make sure this doesn't happen again?**

Well, you could lock her in her room for the next three years. Or you could handcuff yourself to her wrist and make sure she takes you everywhere with her. Not practical? Then your first line of defense is to keep her away from whatever negativity might have sparked this. Get on her Facebook account and see what she and her friends are posting. In my mind, this is not snooping. It's simply getting to know your child better and understanding her social circle. You can weed out the bad seeds better this way. Make sure she's busy after school and on weekends. Busy kids have no time to get into trouble. Encourage her and her friends to "hang" at your home, and make sure there is plenty of V8 Splash and SunnyD and pizza rolls in the freezer.

Even then, you can't be one hundred percent sure it won't happen again. As the mother of a teenage son, I can tell you it's all about the trust factor. Grounding will go only so far. But if your kid trusts you and thinks you're cool, she won't be sneaking around behind your back. Use whatever Jedi mind tricks you can to convince her you're not the bad guy here. You want her to be safe and happy; you want her to realize that you are her friend and she can come to you if she's feeling peer pressure. Parenting is a thankless job, but it's the most important one you could have. I wish you lots of luck, and believe me when I say, I can relate!

**What do you tell a kid who just started middle school and wants to wear makeup? I think it makes her look like a cheap tramp. Isn't she too young?**

In my opinion—and it sounds like yours—this is WAY too early! I'll even get more old school on you: no hair weaves. How do you tell her that? Start with "I'm the grown-up and you're the kid and I still make the rules around here." When she's an adult and starts paying her own bills, she can wear mountains of Maybelline. But until then, while she's under your roof, you call the shots. I understand that young girls have fragile egos, and they want desperately to feel "grown up." But this is middle school—not a glitz pageant. If you must relent, then buy her some clear lip gloss or flavored ChapStick. But if you're asking me, I say keep it real till high school.

**My son is a senior in high school and he's failing. We're not sure he's going to graduate, and he doesn't seem to care. He wants to drop out. I think it's very important that he get his high school diploma. What should I do?**

I don't care about your race, your creed, your color: If you don't have a college degree today, you are on the sidelines of life. And with no high school diploma? You are less than gum on the bottom of the shoe of life. I know people, plenty of people, who have no high school degrees and they have had to doggie-paddle their way to civilization. You do not want your son to be in that position. He's got to graduate high school; there is no other way. And he's so close to that diploma, he can't let it slip through his fingers. If he needs to repeat senior year, he will do it, and you will accept nothing less. Grow a backbone, Mom—I mean that. If you have to make your point heard, then cut off everything that means something to him. No Christmas. No birthday. No car. No cell phone. No Internet service to his iPad. You and your man need to be on the same page about this, and you need to enlist the school's help as well. Get on this boy's case and get him prepared for life. It's your responsibility as a parent—don't drop that ball.

## QUIZ: HOW YOU DOIN'? WHAT KIND OF PARENT ARE YOU?

1. Your child is misbehaving. You:
   a. Bribe him to shut up with a candy bar.
   b. Ask him to "please behave."
   c. Send him to his room for a time-out.

2. Your daughter wants to go to school dressed like a streetwalker. You:
   a. Offer to take her shopping after school if she covers up.
   b. Point out that Beyoncé would not be caught dead in that outfit.
   c. Make her go back and change or be grounded for a week.

3. Your son gets angry and disses you. You:
   a. Offer to make things up to him with tickets to a Jets game.
   b. Tell him he hurt your feelings.
   c. Threaten to wash his mouth out with soap if he ever speaks that way to you again.

4. The assistant principal calls to say your child cut school. You:
   a. Pay him a dollar for every day he stays in school.
   b. Tell him how disappointed you are in his attendance.
   c. Ground him—the only time he will be allowed to leave the house is to go to school.

5. You smell alcohol on your teen's breath. You:
   a. Pour him a glass of top shelf and make sure he can tell the difference.
   b. Warn him that hangovers hurt like a bitch.
   c. Make him go to an AA meeting so he can see what his future might hold.

**If you answered mostly A's:** YOU'RE A PUSHOVER PARENT. I'm all for being a cool parent, but you're spoiling your kid rotten! Stop thinking of yourself as your child's friend. You're his/her parent, and you need to draw some lines and set some rules.

**If you answered mostly B's:** YOU'RE A DIPLOMATIC PARENT. You try to be fair and honest with your child, allowing him/her to make choices as well as mistakes and grow from them. Just make sure you're not a pushover. Being patient and understanding is one thing; being a doormat is another.

**If you answered mostly C's:** YOU'RE A DICTATOR PARENT. Tiger Mom's got nothin' on you! You are strict and often rigid in your parenting. Frankly . . . I don't have a problem with this! If I'm your mama, you treat me with respect. Just know the difference between tough love and bully parenting. Kids need rules and boundaries, but too many threats and punishments can lose their ability to make a point.

• • • • • • • •

**My three-year-old has a mouth like a truck driver! Just the other day, he said "f—k you!" when I said it was bedtime! I think he gets it from his daddy, but I can't make him stop swearing!**

When I was a kid, there was no cursing in my home. My parents didn't tolerate us saying "shut up" much less "FU!" and they had a litany of things that were off-limits. I believe, in a lot of ways, I am a better woman for it, and I am certainly a better parent now. In my house, does my son hear cursing? Yes, he hears it from me. He hears it from his father. I use it when I need to. I use it when I've asked my son to do something five times and he hasn't done it, or when he's really pissed me off.

But he would NEVER swear at us; he knows what hell would descend if he did. He's polite and respectful to his parents and his teachers. Of course, he has picked up a thing or two. You should see some of his texts to his friends: There are four-letter words in there I have never even heard of! Don't tell him I spy on him!

The point is, your son is too young to be using this language. I'm sure he doesn't even know what it means—just that Daddy uses it when he's unhappy or angry. I would talk to your husband and get him in on this. If he's the one who's building your son's vocabulary, then he's the one to do the explaining. Have him tell your toddler that these words are not for children: They're mean and nasty, and they hurt people's feelings. I know: It's a "do as I say, not as I do" kind of lecture, but you'll have a lot more of these down the road as parents. If you hear colorful language coming out of your kid again, punish him. No more playing with LEGOs. No more watching TV. No more treats. He'll get the point.

**I am obese (over three hundred pounds), and I know my daughter is mortified. I overheard her on the phone with her best friend saying how she's embarrassed every time I pick her up from school. I feel so awful . . . what should I do?**

Okay, sister, are you ready for some tough love? It's time for you to lose weight. It's not even about your daughter at this point; it's about you being healthy and happy with the way you look. Obesity is running rampant in our country, and as a former fatty and a woman who fights her weight every day, I sympathize and empathize with you. Not only did I used to be fat, but I'm also five feet eleven inches tall—so I was BIG and FAT. Now I'm just a big girl with a little extra meat on her bones. And I feel better—a lot better. I know you can, too.

You've got to get control of your diet. I don't know how you're going to do it. You should probably talk to your doctor. You might be a candidate for gastric bypass or Lap-Band surgery. A lot of people, like Star Jones, Al Roker, and Lisa Lampanelli, have seen wonderful results. Or if you want to, do it the old-fashioned way: Push back from the table and get into the gym. Listen, losing weight is not a sprint, it's a marathon. It's going to take time to lose this weight, but if your daughter sees you putting in this effort, she'll be proud.

You can't do anything about mean girls. Mean girls will always be mean until you shut them up with being better. And since you feel awful, don't wallow in your guilt and bad feelings. Do something about it!

**Wendy, I strongly suspect that my fifteen-year-old son is gay. I'm okay with it, but my husband isn't. He makes derogatory comments all the time about homosexuals. I don't know if I should confront my son or let him make the decision to come out when he's ready. What would you do?**

With all due respect, your husband is a jerk. I'm nervous for you to say anything to him about this situation. He might flip out and say or do something horrible and hurtful. He could traumatize your kid for life. What I would do and what you should do are two different things, because I am not married to a homophobe. I couldn't live with this man, and I'm not sure how you will continue to do so if your son does come out.

If you strongly suspect that your son is gay, then he probably is. A mother knows. I wouldn't talk to your son about it. I would be the best mother that I can possibly be, including always having an ear ready to listen to his pains and joys in life. And when I tell you that you might have to be prepared to divorce—I'm very serious. Your kid is going to have to deal with a lifetime of discrimination. The last place he should find it is in his home.

**My four-year-old is a spoiled-rotten brat. I hate to say that about my own child, but she is seriously driving me crazy. Everything is "gimme," "I want," "I need," and when she doesn't get it, she throws a tantrum or hits. Help me, Wendy!**

I sincerely hope she is not hitting you—oh, no, that better not be happening! It's time to get ahold of this brat right now. You think a kindergarten teacher is going to put up with this behavior? How about her classmates? Before you know it, you have a friendless little girl sitting in the corner by herself; she won't be invited to birthday parties. You've created this monster and now it's time for you to backpedal. Your daughter needs to get used to hearing the word *no*. Your daughter needs to get used to earning everything that comes her way.

## WENDY'S FINAL WORD
### How to Avoid Kid Drama

- **Practice what you preach.** If you tell your kid "no cursing in our house" that goes for you as well. At least *try* to curb the potty mouth. I know we're grown-ups and we don't have to follow the same rules, but this sends a mixed message to your kid: Do as I say, not as I do.

- **Be involved.** Know what your kid is doing *all the time.* I know you're busy; I know you've got a million things on your plate. But as a parent, you have a responsibility to keep track of whose house your kid is hanging out at and what they're doing behind closed doors. Sometimes it means rearranging your schedule and your priorities, but it's so important.

- **Love them.** Even when they make you want to pull your hair out, love them. And tell them every day.

CHAPTER 8

# WORK DRAMA

I know my job is not good forever. I'm very practical about it. That's the thing with TV—they can always pull the plug! So I ask myself, "What would I want to do next? What's the next chapter in my life?" The biggest mistake most people make at work is staying too long at the fair. You get comfortable. You get lazy. You get complacent. You assume the devil you know is better than the devil you don't. I don't buy that. I believe you always have choices. If your office is fraught with tension and drama, and you are miserable getting up for work every morning, then for God's sake do something about it.

A long time ago, people would collect their gold watch for thirty years of service—but not anymore.

Most people keep moving. How can you get anywhere if you're standing still?

**My boss is always criticizing and insulting me. Last week, she called me stupid. I can't lose my job—I'm a single mom! What should I do?**

I understand that you're in a panic right now—losing your job at this point is not an option. But your boss is dead wrong for telling you you're stupid. A well-thinking person knows how to give constructive criticism without resorting to name-calling. So I want you to think seriously about a Plan B. What else can you do? What are you skilled at? Can you send out résumés or check want ads online? Do you need to take some additional classes? Don't wait for the ax to fall, my friend. Be prepared.

In the meantime, while you are lining all your ducks up in a row, try to keep the peace with your boss. Have a conversation with her that does not end deadly. You have to get back to a place where your boss talks to you like a respectable human being. And if that means sucking up until you have a way out, so be it. You have your kids to think about. Just promise me you will be proactive and find a new place to work where you're not someone's verbal punching bag.

**There's this girl in the office that's a total slut. She's slept her way around the whole department, including with my supervisor. Everyone's talking about her. Should I tell her?**

Hell no—keep your mouth shut! One of the things I am most proud of regarding my whole twenty-five-year career is I never had to sleep with anyone to get to where I am today. But I can rattle off twenty-five or forty names of girls who have slept their way to their positions. I have no respect for them. I don't think anything about them. They do what they do to get to where they need to get, and they have the morals of alley cats (or Monica Lewinsky). But I am also woefully aware that they can take my job at any point. If that happens, all I will have is my integrity intact. That is the way of the world.

Everyone's talking about her? Let them talk. Believe me, she knows and she doesn't care. Girls like this do not deserve to stand next to girls like me and you—and they certainly don't deserve your friendship or sympathy!

**I worked with this guy on a project at work and he took all the credit. My boss has no idea how hard I worked. What should I do?**

You should speak up—sooner rather than later. You don't want to throw your colleague under the bus, but you also don't want to be invisible in your boss's eyes. How would you feel if your coworker got a raise over this and you didn't? Or worse, if they had to make cutbacks and chose to let you go rather than him? Make a formal appointment with your boss and say you'd like to explain your work on this project in better detail. Give specific examples. Hopefully this will teach you a lesson: You need to toot your own horn. There will always be people who don't play fair—beware!

**I think my supervisor made a pass at me. I'm not sure because it was at the holiday party and we were both drinking one or two drinks. I feel awkward now being around him.**

They call alcohol the truth serum for a reason. It loosens our inhibitions, and exposes the truth of who we really are and who we'd really like to be. As far as your boss making a pass at you is concerned, you aren't the first girl this has happened to and you won't be the last. It's called sexual harassment, and you should not simply ignore it. This is your supervisor; he doesn't own the company. He is a working slob like the rest of us. If this working slob ever does this again to you, you want to have all the evidence and proof. Because when all is said and done, he can throw you under the bus and they can fire you from your job. It's him vs. you and you want to win. The only way to win is to be on the defensive. Do not pound drinks back at any more office parties. You want to stay keenly observant, which means observing through sober eyes. And if you need to be around him, make sure you're not alone and there's an open door. He's showed you his hand.

## HOT TOPIC
### What to Do If You're Sexually Harassed at Work

The Equal Rights Association defines sexual harassment as "unwelcome verbal, visual, or physical conduct of a sexual nature." So it's not just your boss copping a feel at the company Christmas party. It can be a guy making a lewd remark ("Nice blouse!") or looking you up and down with drool running out of his mouth. It can be someone of the opposite or even the same sex; the result is always the same. You feel uncomfortable and you want it to stop. Honey, you have rights. You can take action.

- **Don't quit.** I know you want to run for the hills and avoid this scum at all costs. But if you quit your job, you will have no case.

- **Know your rights.** Read your employee handbook—there is always a sexual harassment policy in it. Follow the steps to the letter. If it says to meet with someone (i.e., a higher-up or someone in human resources), then waste no time.

- **Put it in writing.** Every disgusting detail of this dirtbag's behavior. Anything you've experienced or witnessed against you or other employees.

- **Sometimes it's not sexual.** Sometimes you are simply being discriminated against because of your gender. Are you being given lesser assignments? Receiving less pay or commission? Made to work less desirable shifts because you're a woman? You can and should report it.

- **They may not fire the offender.** Believe it or not, according to the law, they don't have to. He may simply be warned or made to take "sensitivity training." Hopefully, they move his ass far away from you to another department to avoid any more conflict.

- **Take it to the next level . . . if the behavior continues.** You can report it to the Equal Employment Opportunity Commission (www.eeoc.gov) or even hire an attorney to sue the bastard and the company.

..................................

**I'm in a dead-end job with no future. I've been working in the same government agency for seven years and I have never gotten a promotion. I don't have a college degree, and I don't think I can get a better position without one.**

Your dead-end job is your dead-end fault. And I'm saying it like that. I've always billed myself as a hustler, a person who is one step ahead of what the boss has to say regarding where my future goes. The idea that you have been in the same job for seven years and you have no future? Listen, that was your decision. You could have gone to school and earned a college degree—or at the very least gotten your junior college degree, which is two years. You don't think you can get another position because you have no confidence in yourself. So, yeah, I'm blaming this on you. I hate to talk tough, but if you're thinking you have no future, you probably don't. Because you don't believe in it.

What should you do? Go back to school. Not full-time, but part-time. You need to better your education, maybe take some specialty courses to get you on the fast track to being proficient in a field you like. You don't need to share with anyone that you haven't gotten a promotion in seven years. This is an abomination. An embarrassment. Where is your backbone?

Now I've used the word *backbone* a lot in this book because I feel that a lot of you need to rely on yourself. I can't help you until you help yourself. I suggest that you fire up your life on twenty-five cylinders and get it together. Everything's got to change, including your attitude.

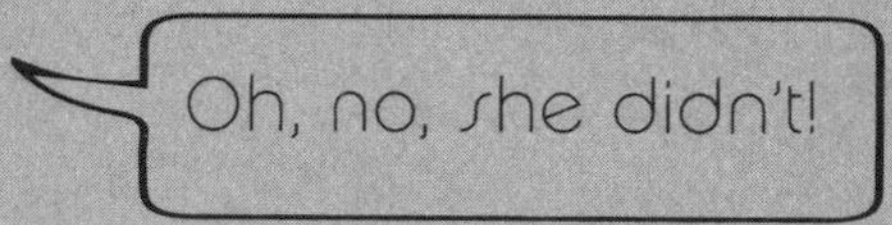


**My coworker is always making personal calls. We share a cubicle and she's on the phone all day, bitching at her boyfriend. She even called her gyno once and spoke to her about genital warts. Seriously, Wendy, TMI. How do I get her to shut up?**

Tell her: "Sweetie, could you keep the details of your vagina to yourself?" If you share a cubicle, then apparently she's your equal. In an effort to keep the peace, you might want to pull out a thesaurus and pick kind words and speak to her diplomatically. Give it three months and see how/if it changes. If it doesn't, go to the boss.

**I got a raise. My best friend at work didn't. She asked me if I'd gotten one, and I kind of lied to her and said no. Now I feel weird.**

Don't feel weird; this is competition. This is part of the reason why back in the girlfriend drama chapter, I took a pretty hard line. I learned early the difference between saving my own ass and saving a friendship that could one day mean absolutely nothing to me. Your girlfriend at work is not paying your bills.

It's also none of her business if you got a raise. Even if she sees that you bought a beautiful couch from Neiman Marcus or a hot pair of Louboutins, it's none of her business how you were able to afford them. I don't condone lying, but she put you on the spot. You better stop feeling weird about this. You done good, girl. Enjoy your raise and the praise, and don't give this girlfriend a second thought.

**My husband hates his job as a contractor and wants to quit. He thinks I should go back to work as a maid, which I hate. And he'll stay home all day and sit on his ass. He says we have no family, so it's not a problem to "take a break."**

Oh, no, he will not. If you had kids, and he wanted to do the whole Mr. Mom thing, I'd say maybe. But since you don't, it's not his right to leave a job he hates and stick you in one that you hate. Hundreds of thousands of millions of people in this country hate their jobs. Just because you hate it doesn't mean you can quit it. It sounds like you both need to reconsider your careers, and this should be done fairly and squarely. Sit down and talk over how you are going to make some changes. Maybe he trains weekends or nights for a new career, and keeps his old one until he has some other offers. And you start looking in the want ads for a new profession to help support the household.

One day, you may have a family, and this will not be an option. You'll have hungry mouths to feed. Do it now, do it for yourselves, and do it for each other.

**I'm thirty and single and have no kids. I know I'm in the wrong profession. I hate being a bookkeeper. I want to go back to school and study nursing. Do you think it's too late? My parents say I'm crazy.**

Under other circumstances, I would say you're crazy, too. For example, if you were responsible for a family, this might not be the best decision. But since the lane is clear for you to do whatever you want to do, I say, "Do it." Go back to school. Become a nurse. Keep your job as a bookkeeper because that's what's paying for your nursing classes, but take courses at night or online.

As far as your parents are concerned, make their words to you white noise. You're not asking them for money, are you? You don't need them to babysit. Parents often tell you you're crazy about your career choice. (Mine sure did.) It took my TV show to make them understand, "Aw, Wendy was right." To them, anything out of the norm is stupid. But you know better. You know it's smart and gutsy, and the way to go.

**My boss called me into her office and said someone had complained about my attitude to her. I have no idea who ratted me out or what they said, but I am going to kill whoever said it.**

Using the words *ratted* and *kill* suggest to me that you might indeed be sporting some 'tude. I think what you need to do is check it when you come in the door to your workplace. Your attitude is not going to get you a raise, and it's not going to get you brownie points. Do not go confusing being a bitch with being a fierce leader.

I don't think you should be asking me, "What should I do?" Instead, how about "What did I do?" to compel your boss to call you into her office? And how are you going to clean it up?

Stop worrying your pretty head about who dropped dime on you. Instead, make an appointment with your boss and find out what was said. Was it a specific situation . . . or a general complaint? Explain that you want to be a team player and you are willing to make whatever changes need to be made. You have coworkers, and you have to cowork with them. If you're not, then I suggest you get your résumé ready.

## QUIZ: HOW YOU DOIN'? WHAT KIND OF AN EMPLOYEE ARE YOU?

Are you a diligent team player . . . or a kiss-ass complainer? Employees come in all shapes and styles. Answer the questions honestly, and check your score below.

1. Your boss suggests that from now on, everyone comes to work on holidays and Saturdays. You:
   a. Smile and say, "Great idea, chief!"
   b. Take a survey of your coworkers: How do they feel about it?
   c. Ask him what crack he's been smoking lately . . . what a stupid idea!

2. You have nothing to do at work. You:
   a. Offer to clean your boss's office—and maybe his shoes need buffing?
   b. Ask any of your coworkers if they need help on a project.
   c. Play a few rounds of solitaire on your computer to pass the time.

3. A new person is joining your office team. You:
   a. Buy her lunch . . . and make sure your boss sees your generous gesture.

b. Give him the tour and introduce him around.

c. Google him. Get as much dirt as you can.

4. One of your coworkers is having marriage troubles and can't concentrate. You:

a. Bring this to your supervisor's attention: No one needs a weak link.

b. Offer to take her out for a drink after work and take her mind off it.

c. Ask if her husband is interested in dating yet . . . you have a single friend who'd be perfect for him!

5. Your boss asks if you want to take on a complicated new project. You:

a. Hug him and tell him he's made your dreams come true.

b. Ask him if you might have a few people to work with you on it; the more great minds, the better.

c. Tell him, "Gee, that sounds great! Almost as much fun as a root canal!"

**If you answered mostly A's:** YOU ARE A BOOTLICKER. Your boss says jump and you say "how high?" Have some dignity! This approach to climbing the work ladder won't work in the long run. No one respects a spineless brownnoser.

**If you answered mostly B's:** YOU ARE A PEOPLE PLEASER. You want to earn the trust and admiration of your coworkers and supervisors, so you do your best to be considerate, fair, and a friend to all. Unlike the bootlicker, you're sincere. Just make sure people don't take advantage of your kind nature.

**If you answered mostly C's:** YOU ARE THE OFFICE A-HOLE. I hate to say it, but if you have this much 'tude, no one is going to want to work with you. Where do you get off? Mouthing off to your superiors is not the way to succeed in business—unless you're trying to get fired. (In which case, you're doing an excellent job!)

• • • • • • • •

Oh, no, she didn't!

**My boss just had a baby and thinks it's totally fine to breast-feed in the office. I think it's gross and inappropriate. I walked in on her the other day and saw her boob. Am I supposed to just ignore it?**

Yes, you are. But personally, I think she's taking advantage of people's tolerance. I have no problem with public breast-feeding when it's an emergency situation. Your breasts are engorged or your baby is screaming to be fed. By all means, breast-feed. But your boss seems to be making an intentional declaration of her mothering. Because if you are in the workplace, that means there is a bathroom. And if you are in the bathroom, there is usually a bathroom stall. She could also lock the door to her office so an unsuspecting employee won't barge in and get an eyeful. She has done none of the above. So I think you need to be the one who is on guard. Knock. Shield your eyes. Call first. Make it sound like you're being super considerate, not avoiding another "tit-illating" situation.

**My office is relocating to another state. I've lived here my whole life, and my friends and family don't want me to go. I am a single mother with a toddler, and I don't think I have a choice. Advice please?**

If I listened to my friends and family and paid attention to where they were geographically located, I would never have had the *Wendy Williams* TV show. I would never have had my radio show, and I would have been stuck with a bunch of complacent people. So I say ignore the voices in your head and those from your family and your friends. This is about you as a single mother and putting food on the table for you and your child. In life, there are a lot of things we don't want to do. It's time for you to move on and make your way. You will make new friends and Skype the old ones. Please don't let being comfortable be the reason you jeopardize your future. It's time to grow up and leave the nest. Now.

**I have lots of health issues: asthma, gallbladder, kidney stones, etc., and I had to take several sick days this year. My boss gave me a warning and I'm worried he's going to fire me.**

I'm sorry to say, but he probably will. Your boss is under the gun to get the best players into position to make the company look good. I am so sorry for your health issues. If you are worried he is going to fire you, then you must have a suspicion that you are on his radar. Can you play "well"? Can you not take off for any little things, only the big ones? Make sure you get a doctor's note for every sick day to cover your ass. And in the meantime, I'd get an attorney. You need to investigate the legal ramifications of what your boss is doing to you and what recourse you have. This is a very, very difficult but common situation that many people are in right now. You have rights, and there is something called the Family Medical Leave Act that protects an employee who is incapacitated by a serious illness. Do the best you can do, and take care of you.

## WENDY'S FINAL WORD
### How to Have Less Drama at Work

- **No friends at work.** Sorry to sound so cold, but as a woman who has had to scrap and scrape her way through the workplace, I will tell you they never work or last. You can have mutually respectful acquaintances or people you go to lunch with. Just don't go sharing your deepest, darkest secrets with anyone who is on the payroll.

- **No lovers at work.** Yes, I met my first husband at work and married him—and look how well that turned out (see chapter two). No matter how cute he or she is, try to do better; it is not worth the aggravation or the potential aftermath. Do not shit where you eat. These are words I live by.

- **Dress the part.** Don't dress for the job you have, dress for the job you want. So when Casual Fridays come and everyone is wearing sloppy jeans, you look put together. No rips. No Rolling Stones T-shirt. Sleek and chic. It's the best way to be taken seriously.

- **Keep your computer clean.** Stay off Facebook, Twitter, tumblr. Do not be IMing your boyfriend. Big Brother is probably watching—and if not him, then your coworkers. This is considered pilfering company equipment for personal use, and companies do not go easy on it anymore.

- **Move in silence.** Do not share what you are doing with your coworkers or your bosses. It's nice to make small talk at the watercooler, but don't inform them about your weekend plans, your fight with your boyfriend, your STD. Seriously: only need-to-know info. Keep your personal life personal before it comes back to bite you in the ass. And it will. Someone will inevitably share whatever info you gave out and the whole office will know you have crabs.

# CHAPTER 9

# NEIGHBOR DRAMA

When I was growing up in Ocean Township, New Jersey, we lived across the street from the Radzutskys and the McDonaughs. Everybody was in the same house for thirty years period and we knew these people intimately. It doesn't happen like that anymore. Neighbors come, neighbors go. Not everyone is Mr. Rogers singing "Won't You Be My Neighbor?" Some people are downright ornery and inconsiderate. Sometimes you're the offender and you don't even know it!

We had a situation recently at our house: Our property is pitched on a hill, and a tree fell in a neighbor's yard. The roots were clearly on our side, but it was on a part of the property that we don't normally stare at, so I had no idea it had happened. It had apparently lain there for at least a month and we had done nothing. One day, our next-door neighbor ding-donged and pointed it out, and asked me to haul it out of there. We are not great friends, so I considered this to be friendly fire. I immediately called our landscaper and told him to remove it. Then I sent a muffin basket with an "I'm sorry" note. We're good. Never underestimate the power of a muffin basket if your neighbor is causing problems . . .

**My neighbor next door in our apartment building is a pig. She leaves shoes, umbrellas, even kids' bicycles in the hall. When I told her to take it inside, she said I could stick it.**

Not that I'm defending anyone leaving their shit on someone else's turf, but it is not unusual for a busy mom in a crowded apartment to leave shoes, umbrellas, and bicycles in the hallway. These things in the hall make for more space inside the apartment. She's not going to change, because she can't. Her apartment is small. And her reaction should tell you she doesn't want it. Until you move to a better situation, whether it's a detached house or an apartment building that has storage in the basement, there is not much you can do. Except maybe one thing . . .

Talk to your landlord, anonymously. Let him know the apartment number and the floor where all these things are sitting in the hall. Let him be the bad guy. Maybe he'll buy an umbrella tree or some shoe bins and make things look a little tidier. I'd tell you to stop aggravating yourself and just worry about your own space. It's not worth it.

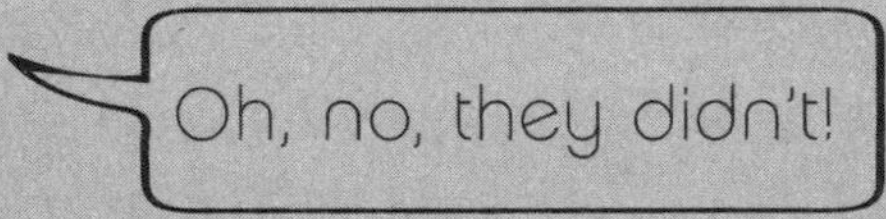


**The people who live above us are having some crazy animal sex all night long. I hear moaning, panting, and bed banging. It's driving me nuts. Help!**

Sexual sound effects are not fun unless they're happening in your own boudoir. I would bake a pie or buy some cookies and go upstairs, gift in hand, and have a little talk. It might be awkward because it's about their sex life, but don't dance around the issue. If you are old enough to have your name on a lease, then you are old enough and mature enough to talk to your neighbor sensibly and directly about what is bothering you. But if you just can't bear the confrontation, you can always play dumb: "I have no idea what all the commotion could be, but I'm hearing a lot of noise from your apartment late at night. Is there something you can do to quiet it down?" Hopefully, they'll muffle the moaning from now on and let you get some sleep!

**This woman next door is an old lady, and I feel bad saying it, but her apartment stinks. I can smell it every time she opens her door and it makes me sick. I know she can't get out much and has health issues . . . should I tell someone or get a gas mask?**

Tell the landlord and your superintendent. Don't get me wrong: I am not hating on the old lady. Oftentimes, elderly people are too frail to open windows and let fresh air in. They can't make it to the incinerator with old newspapers or the trash, and they can't get out to the store and buy some Febreze. This doesn't seem like a volatile situation, so I don't think you have to hide the fact that you're doing the complaining. Horrible stinky smells are sometimes more than horrible stinky smells. They are health hazards. You have every right to have the situation checked out and rectified. Please don't feel guilty.

**My neighbor got a puppy and our building doesn't allow pets. The thing keeps yapping and whining all day, so someone is bound to find out. I feel like I should tell the super, but my neighbor is a nice lady and I don't want to rat her out. What should I do?**

I love dogs. I grew up with three dogs and two bunny rabbits. But if the building does not permit pets, your neighbor has no right to harbor a fluffly little friend. As nice as she may be, I would complain to the super and I would complain loud and proud. I would also find out who lives on the other side of this person and across the hall. They have to be hearing the same yips and yaps as you. There is safety in numbers. Think of it this way: If you were in your apartment puffing away on a cigarette in a no-smoking building, people would be complaining about you. I feel for pets, but this woman has broken the rules of the building. She needs to send her pup elsewhere or move out.

**The guy down the hall likes to smoke cigars and the smell is unbearable. He says he can do anything he wants—it's his apartment—but I can smell it all the way in mine. How do I get him to stop?**

Guess what? There is no sign on the wall that says this is a no-smoking building. You have complained to this guy. You've come to no resolution. My suggestion to you would be to go out and get the best HEPA filters to clean the air, and the best screens for your windows. Open those windows wide. When we smoked our weed and our cigars in college, we would put a wet towel at the crack/base of the front door and it would act as a filter and absorb the smell. You might try the same trick to keep his cigar stink from invading your place. But there is nothing else you can do. The guy is right: He can smoke if he wants in his apartment. I hope the next time you move into a place, you "nose" better and you make sure it's a no-smoking building!

## QUIZ: HOW YOU DOIN'? ARE YOU THE NEIGHBOR FROM HELL?

I'm not pointing any fingers . . . but you know what you do and how you behave. Take this quiz and rate your good or bad neighborly-ness.

1. You bought a mattress for your bedroom. You put the old one:
   a. In your neighbor's driveway till you can figure out what to do with it.
   b. On your front lawn—the kids will love using it as a trampoline.
   c. In the garbage and called someone to come haul it right away.

2. You smell smoke coming from the next-door apartment. You:
   a. Assume they burned dinner and ignore it.
   b. Call and leave a message on their machine: "Is something burning over there?"
   c. Ring the doorbell, and if no one answers, get the super to check and make sure they're okay.

3. Your dog took a dump on your neighbor's lawn. You:
   a. Give Fido a reward for his excellent aim.

b. Leave it alone and hope they won't notice . . . or step in it.
c. Scoop the poop before they find out.

4. Your kids trample your neighbor's flower bed with their bikes. You:
a. Make sure not a single rose remains.
b. Hide the bikes in the garage—they can't accuse you without evidence!
c. Make your munchkins apologize and offer to pay for replanting.

5. Your neighbor has been feeling under the weather and her landscaping is a mess. You:
a. Snap pics of her gnarly bushes and burned grass and post them on Facebook.
b. Put a fence around your property so you don't have to look at it.
c. Offer to have your teenage son do some yard work for a small fee.

**If you answered mostly A's:** Damn, I hope you never ring my bell! Why so antagonistic? Even if they let their dog poop on your lawn all the time, you're not making things any better. Take the higher road.

**If you answered mostly B's:** You like to mind your own business and stay out of everybody else's. This isn't a bad policy; it's just not going to win you any popularity contest in your hood. Just make sure you're laissez-faire attitude isn't being construed as negligence.

**If you answered mostly C's:** You get the gold star for neighborhood nice guy. But you know my opinion on this—you don't need to be best buds with all the people on your block. Cordial, yes, but don't offer to babysit their kids or walk their dog. Trust me, they'll use and abuse you because they can.

• • • • • • • •

## The house next door has a broken alarm that keeps going off and waking us at night. We've nicely and politely asked them to fix it, and nada.

Every time my alarm goes off and the situation doesn't warrant it, we get a seventy-five-dollar ticket from the town police department. It's happened to me twice over the years, and the cops come and they're pissed. Trust me: It made me call the alarm company the next day and check it out.

You've tried resolving this yourself and it's not working. So if I were you, I would go to the police and have them put the screws to this woman. Get the law on your side! They will make note of every time her alarm sounds, and eventually, she will get tired of paying tickets and get it fixed. What she is doing falls under the heading "disturbing the peace," and trust me when I say the men in blue will not let her get away with it.

**A nut job moved to our block. I say this because she sits on her porch, chanting and doing yoga. The other day she was walking to the mailbox on the corner in nothing but a baby-doll nightie. What's up with that?**

There are always going to be people in your neighborhood whom you don't particularly care for. So you're not thrilled with this woman's lifestyle. If you don't like it, move. Until then, you can drop subtle hints. I'd march myself over there with a muffin basket and find out what she's all about. Maybe she's a yoga instructor or a Buddhist monk? When it gets colder, she'll move her practice inside. And the next time you spot her walking down the street in her skivvies, play the part of the cautious, concerned friend: "Do you think it's safe for you to be walking around like this?" Nutty or not, this person is part of your hood. Try to find the humor in the situation: Sounds like she could be more entertaining to watch than a sitcom!

**I'm convinced I live next door to one of those hoarders from TV. Seriously, I went over one day to deliver a package that accidentally came to my house and she opened the door and you couldn't see in, there was so much crap. I know it's none of my business, but I think it's a fire hazard.**

It's not just a fire hazard, because a lot of other "things" are probably living in her hoards of crap. Like vermin. Like bedbugs. We're talking health hazard here. Hoarding is nasty and unsanitary, and when it gets out of control, it affects the entire community. No one is safe with this situation. Eventually, it will even affect property values, because when people find out that they are buying a house in a neighborhood with a hoarder, they will run. So I am on your team with this.

Call the health department. They will handle it from there. They will not let up. They'll make her clean up her act or else.

**My neighbor is always "borrowing" things from me, like batteries, milk, and sugar, or change for the laundry, etc. It's beginning to get on my nerves. What should I do?**

You should stop lending. Batteries are expensive. So is milk; so is sugar. Change for the laundry? No, ma'am. Nickels and quarters add up to dollars. Dollars add up to your retirement fund. Do not lend another thing. Simply tell your neighbor that you don't have any of the above. Every time your doorbell rings, you tell her you are out of whatever thing she wants. There is no need to be nasty; in fact, you can sound all apologetic-like. After the third or fourth try, she'll stop and find another borrowing buddy.

**A total hottie moved into my apartment building. We met in the elevator. He's a volunteer firefighter . . . need I say more? Is it totally stupid**

**for me to show some neighborliness or is a hookup with someone in your building a bad idea? Any advice?**

And your idea of neighborliness is jumping between his legs? I see where your mind is going here . . . straight to his crotch. Look, it's not advisable (if you have a falling out, he'll be in close proximity), no matter how hot-hot-hot he is. Hooking up with a neighbor is much like hooking up with a coworker. In my opinion, it always ends up ugly. So I would tell you to fantasize about your fireman but refrain from anything that involves you and him igniting your own flames.

## HOT TOPIC
### Avoiding Neighbor Drama

Neighbors come, neighbors go. But we all have one common goal: to live in peace and harmony. Here's how:

- **Courtesy goes a long way.** My husband and I leave the house very early to go to the TV studio in Manhattan, sometimes when it's still dark out and our neighbors are sleeping. So we leave the headlights off on the car until we get to the end of the driveway—no one would appreciate bright lights shining in their bedroom as a wake-up call. It's that simple: Be considerate. If by chance, the dry-cleaning service drops off a suit that was for next door, walk it over. Think of how you would want to be treated and treat your neighbors with the same care and respect.

- **Give them a heads-up.** If you are throwing a big party at your place, make sure your next-door neighbors know that it might be loud and late. Give them a card with your phone number: Call me if the noise is too much. Don't call the cops, call me! They'll appreciate the warning. Heck, maybe they'll even get out of town for the weekend!

- **Keep your property up.** Please God! Don't be the bum-ass house on the block. Keep your lawn mowed, your leaves raked, your kids' crap out of the driveway. When our garbage cans are empty, the wind sometimes whips up and blows them down the street. Do you think we let them stay there? We race out and gather them up so we don't give anyone a reason to complain.

- **Don't share service people.** I've learned from experience. My lawn-care company is not the same as my neighbors'. My plumber is not the same. Why? Because service and repair people are nothing but gossips. You get to know them while they are fixing your fridge and you say, "So what's going on next door?" And they tell you everything. They also take your information and spread it around on their next call: "Yeah, the outside of the house looks beautiful, but inside it's a mess. There are holes in the wall. The furniture is terrible. She's a hoarder." Whatever. The Roto-Rooter dude and the Maytag repairman have big mouths. If you want your business to be your own, then don't share your source for repairs.

# CHAPTER 10

# ONLINE DRAMA

I have a love/hate relationship with Facebook. I love it because you can keep up with your friends and what's going on with their lives and they can follow your news. When I'm busy, it's convenient and it eliminates hours on the phone "catching up." What I hate about it is that it gets in the way of real relationships. It complicates things, and relationships are complicated enough.

I grew up with face-to-face conversation—none of this texting and e-mailing or Skyping stuff. We sat down over coffee or a cocktail and chewed the fat. Technology makes communication easier and faster, but it also makes it less personal. I need to sit down with my son and my husband and ask them, "How was your day?" Could I e-mail or text it? Sure. But it's not the same.

And the way things come across in texts can easily be misunderstood. You can't tell if someone is joking or teasing in a post. You can't read their body language or their facial expressions. For that reason alone, I am a big believer that the minute you are in a serious relationship, you take a break from online chatter. Don't post your relationship-status updates. Don't look at your boyfriend's wall and try to figure out which girls he was dating before you. Take a tech time-out and give your relationship the attention it deserves and needs. I know, you're thinking I'm a fifty-year-old fuddy-duddy for saying this. But I believe it: Social networks can screw up your relationship faster than you can say, "IM me!"

**My new boyfriend un-friended me on Facebook. He said it's because his guy friends say rude stuff all the time. But I'm not sure. Do you think he's hiding something?**

Darling, I'm not sure. I'm fifty-fifty on this one because guys do say rude stuff—immature guys. But Facebook is a great place to believe you can hide things.

If he's your boyfriend, he should want to share. Tell him you're a big girl; you're familiar with boy talk and it won't faze you. If he still refuses, then I would think twice. What else is he going to hide from you if your relationship gets more serious? There needs to be a policy of full disclosure, both on Facebook and beyond.

**My friend tagged me on these high school photos on Facebook. I was fat and pimply in high school, and the last thing I want is for people to see me like that! I swear, she's doing it on purpose!**

I don't want to believe your friend is a mean girl. Does she really know how upset you are? Does she respect your feelings? Unless the photos are pornographic, copyrighted, or in violation of Facebook's terms of use, administrators will not remove them from your friend's profile. You can untag them on yours, but they'll still be out there. Have a conversation with your friend. Ask her politely to please cease and desist. In the meantime, I want you to take a good, hard look in the mirror. Look how far you've come! You're not that girl anymore. Be proud. Honey, weren't we all fat and pimply in high school? Do you really think people are going to look at these old pics and think any less of you? My high school photos are pretty awful, but I own up to the person I was and the person I've become. I suggest you stop worrying about the past and focus on your fab future.

**My boyfriend found out I was two-timing him and it was ugly. We're both twenty-five, and we've been dating since grad school. He took some videos of me half naked and drunk back then, and now he's threatening to put them on YouTube to get back at me. I'm afraid to break up with him for fear of what he might do!**

Welcome to the crazy cyberworld we live in, where you can make a mistake and someone can be an ass and post it for the world to see. How many celebs have wound up with unwanted publicity because some ass of an ex did this to them? I always tell girls (particularly women who are single and having a good time): Never fall asleep naked. You don't know who you can trust these days.

I'm going to address you one subject at a time. First of all, you're two-timing. Things happen. You're twenty-five. When a guy does it, society just chalks it up to him being a man. You don't get that kind of break. Women who cheat are branded with the Scarlet Letter. And that's where your boyfriend is coming from: He's pissed; he hates you for hurting his pride. He can't get beyond it. Guess what? Whether you stay with him or not, if he wants to put raunchy videos of you on YouTube, he will. You can't stay with him and placate him just because he's blackmailing you. The relationship is over; it was probably done for way before this episode. If you were cheatin', you were not happy.

I don't know what you do for a living. Certainly something like this can come back to haunt you. See if you can get your hands on the video. How bad is it exactly? Is there a boob hanging out? Is there crotch showing? Or are you just in a T-shirt and panties? Look, you made this bed. You're going to have to lie in it. Just please learn from it and don't allow yourself to get caught with your pants down again.

**My college roommate thinks it's funny to tweet embarrassing stuff about me. Today she wrote that I was on the rag, and yesterday she said I got drunk and puked in the dorm hallway. It's none of her business and I don't need her announcing it. What do I do?**

Your roommate has stepped over the line so many times that I can't wait for the end of the semester so you can change. Talk to your RA now and get those wheels in motion! Look, you're in college. Things happen. I've been there and done it. I've got millions of stories to tell you about my very own puking in the hallway. Difference is nobody was tweeting it. I'm not sure what her rationale is. If I had to bet, I'd say she's jealous, and she's trying to take you down a notch. The worse she makes you look, the better she looks.

You have to speak to her. When you do, try to control your anger. Practice it in front of the mirror a few times if you need to. The gist of what you are going to tell her is that you do not appreciate her tweeting the goings-on in your life. You are a private person, and because you share a space, she is privy to what's going on in your life. You expect her to respect your wishes and your privacy. If she doesn't, then go to your RA or another dorm official and complain. Her behavior is not funny or acceptable.

**My husband complains that I am addicted to Facebook. He says I'm online all the time talking to my friends instead of paying attention to him. Give me a break!**

I must tell you, if your husband made this observation, there's probably something to it. You probably are on Facebook a lot, and perhaps he's worried that you're gossiping or venting about him. You can't overlook communication and nurturing in your marriage. When you do, it's the beginning of the end. So what I will say to you is: Block off a particular amount of time every day and that's your Facebook-ing time. It should be no longer than forty-five minutes or one solid hour. Time yourself and get off when that time is up. And give your hubby a little more attention. Watch a movie or TV show together. Go out for dinner. Cook him his favorite Sunday breakfast. Make him feel wanted and needed . . . not just a break between posts . . .

**Wendy, I'm furious. My fifteen-year-old daughter put inappropriate pictures of her and her friends on Facebook. Skimpy clothes and sexy poses! I threatened to pull her account, but she says all kids do this stuff. What should I do?**

Pull her account and pull it as of yesterday. Don't even give her a date or time for when you plan on turning it back on. This is a five-alarm fire, and you need to put it out. Your child has shown you that she is not mature enough to be on Facebook. My Kevin is twelve, and all of his friends in seventh grade have Facebook accounts. He knows he is not getting one until we say so. *N-O.* But even when we do allow him, I want all the passwords. I want to see what he is writing and whom he is talking to. I want to know every photo he puts on his wall. This is a nonnegotiable in my home. I wish you luck, because your daughter is going to be extremely unhappy. She may even try to open an account behind your back. Warn her of the repercussions. Her ass will be grounded for the rest of her life and monks in monasteries will get to go to more parties than she does. She has to earn your respect and your trust before you will ever let her back online again.

## HOT TOPIC
### Cyber-Safety

Having a social network is fun . . . but it can also be dangerous. From phishing to identity theft, a crook can learn anything and everything about you from what you blab online.

- **Change your passwords.** Often. And don't make them something totally obvious, like your last name or the last four digits of your social security number. It doesn't take a genius to figure that one out! And don't give them out to anyone.

- **Never e-mail important info.** Like your credit-card number, your bank accounts, the combination to your safe-deposit box. I don't care if it's your hubby who is asking. Never over the Internet, where any savvy hacker can tap into it.

- **Never post what you don't want the world to see.** Sure, you think no one is going to watch your YouTube channel. Then all of a sudden it goes viral 'cause you've made such an ass of yourself.

- **Remember that once you post, it's tough to take it back.** You can delete, but chances are it's already out there. Read and reread before you press send.

- **Everyone will know your business.** If you post your current résumé on LinkedIn, if you include your phone, e-mail, and address on your Facebook profile, you are inviting people to find you. In my opinion, the less said, the better. If they want to know, then ask them to message you privately. Maybe I'm a paranoid woman who works in New York, but I just assume there are creeps lurking around every corner who are waiting for me to let loose these kind of details.

- **Limit and manage who can see your photos and profile.** I'd restrict this to only your closest family and friends. Not some guy you met at the supermarket checkout.

.......................................

**An ex found me on Facebook and sent me a friend request. Is it a bad idea to friend him? It's not like I'm giving him my phone number.**

It depends on why he's your ex. If he was abusing you, cursing you out, and hitting you, then he's an ex for a reason, and no, it's not a good idea. He should be dead to you, including on Facebook. But if it was just that you broke up for irreconcilable differences, then sure. Why not? It doesn't mean that you're going to date him again. Just keep an eye on that un-friend button. He may be friending you to scope out what you're doing and who you are doing it with. I've been known to "snoop" on Facebook in the past; it's a great way to spy on someone. Don't assume his reasons are all friendly . . .

**My husband stays in touch with his exes on Facebook. He says it's not cheating, but it makes me really pissed. What should I do?**

Tell your husband it's either them or you. That's right: I said it. And any one of you who is reading this right now and calling me insecure, guess what? It's not being insecure. It's living and learning and knowing that an ex is supposed to be "ex-communicated" and "expelled" from your daily doings. Your husband has got to put himself in your position. What if your exes came along and you started friending them? And you said, "Oh! it's not cheating!" Would he like that? Doubt it. I don't like that your husband is being so cavalier about something that is bothering you and me so much. This right here is a little battle that needs to be fought. I hope that your husband respects your wishes. You don't need anyone around in his life who knows his ecstasy face. Okay?

**Is it wrong to check my husband's e-mails? I know his password. I kind of want to know whom he's talking to when he's up late working on his laptop.**

Girl, I'm going to be brutal and tell you YES! It's okay to check his e-mails. If you're suspicious, if something is making the hairs on the back of your neck stand on end, then I think you should listen to your female instincts and search his in-box. That said, I don't think you should make this a constant habit. It will create a tremendous amount of distrust if he finds out. Then he'll want to check your e-mails and it will get ugly. Have a look-see, and if all looks fine, then put your mind at ease. Please!

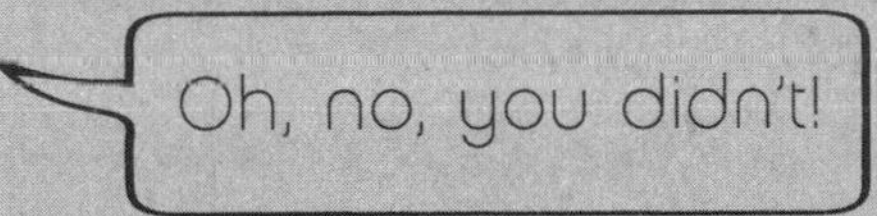


**I got arrested in college a few years ago for an antifur protest on campus. When people Google me, it comes up. Pics and all. I'm terrified some guy I meet and get serious with will see it.**

Listen: "If you don't stand for something, you'll fall for anything." I am proud of you for standing up for something and taking time out of your day to picket and protest. Good for you. Don't be embarrassed by it. Any boyfriend who is not down with the salt of who you are is not boyfriend material.

For now, put it out of your head. You'll deal with it when the time comes, because I'm sure the time will come. It's not something you have to mention or bring up until he's your boyfriend. We all have skeletons in our closets. Google just makes them a lot easier to find . . .

## How truthful should I be on my online dating profile?

I think you should be very truthful. The most important thing is that you post pictures that reflect who you really are. There is nothing wrong with cheating the angle or retouching here and there. But don't "invent" a persona. Don't post a pic of Tyra Banks and claim that it's you. Don't say that you're a lawyer when you're a paralegal. There is creative embellishment . . . then there is telling whoppers!

You can always use fancier words for things you might not want to reveal in such a direct way. For instance, if you mop floors for a living, say that you are a "maintenance engineer," which is the same thing as a janitor. If you are not the exact size that you want to be (maybe you're carrying an extra twenty-five pounds around your hips and you're still working on that), then crop the picture from the waist up. Don't be concerned with every detail—just the important ones.

## WENDY'S FINAL WORD

### How to Avoid Online Drama

- **Never say in a text, e-mail, or post something you would never say to someone's face.**

- **Online communication can be easily misconstrued.** Even if you use one of those emoticons, how do I know if you're saying something in jest or being serious? Before you freak, make sure you have the whole story.

- **Don't hide behind a cyber-mask.** It's easy to sit at your computer and be someone else. No one sees you, right? Be honest—the truth will always get out and bite you in the ass.

- **Don't become an online addict.** Monitor the number of hours you are spending at your computer, on social media, etc. If it's getting in the way of you living your life (i.e., you haven't left the house in three days), then pull the plug.

## CHAPTER 11

# BODY IMAGE DRAMA

My mother and father put me on my first diet in first grade. I grew up being told by my dad, "Wendy, you have such a pretty face . . . if you would just lose some weight . . ." I was never allowed seconds of anything. I had a weekly "weigh-in" day. My parents would tell me to strip down to my T-shirt and panties and make me step on a scale every Friday until I was in the tenth grade. I learned how to manipulate the numbers: I knew that if I set the scale on the bathroom floor mat, I would weigh about two pounds less. If I leaned harder on my right heel, I would be about five pounds less.

I used to hate back-to-school shopping. My mother would sit there on the bench making faces as she watched me peel off my clothes. She would criticize the way I looked and tug on the clothes: "Oh my gosh, you've gained weight since last September! Now here you are in the bigger size!" I would bribe my brother to sneak me Twinkies and tell my mom he ate them, not me. I would eat all the cake and candy I could get my hands on and drop the wrappers behind my bed so my parents didn't know. I was such a wreck over my weight, that I wet my bed till I was twelve.

I know that all of this sounds cruel, but I have forgiven my parents and I love them. If they hadn't sounded the weight alarm back then, I would have probably kept on eating. So maybe they did me a favor? If they hadn't put on the brakes, I might be an obese woman today. I'm not sure. But what I do know is that the weight issue did a huge number on my head.

When I look in the mirror now, I am constantly critical of my body. There, I shared it with you. *Constantly* critical. Right now I weigh 175 pounds and I am five eleven, and I think that my body looks terrific five out of seven days a week. But I've had several surgeries to get to this place. I had large-volume liposuction in 1994. I had my breasts done because I had an A cup on one side and a B cup on the other. And after I had my son, I followed up with a tummy tuck because I gained 103 pounds. When I get out of the shower, I always pinch and pull to see where I can do better. I go to the gym twice a week. I work out very hard with my trainer. I am always counting calories—right down to condiments. I'd rather eat mustard than mayonnaise because mustard has no calories.

I can see a lot of you nodding your heads right now. Oh, yeah—this sounds familiar! Judging from the amount of questions I got on this topic, I know there are many of you out there dealing with body image drama. We need to be honest with ourselves. I say fix what you can and deal with the rest. Let me tell you, it might take you a full fifty years (like me) to become right with your body, but do the best you can.

**I think my twenty-two-year-old daughter has an eating disorder. When I ask her about it, she says to leave her alone and that she's not a baby anymore. She's trying to be an actress and says the camera adds ten pounds. I know she resents me for interfering, but I'm worried. What should I do?**

Start by telling your daughter that you love her and that her body is fine. But I'll be honest with you: No matter how much positive reinforcement you give her, she is being influenced by the outside world. She sees these actresses on TV and in the movies and on magazine covers, airbrushed to death, and that is what she thinks is beautiful. Eating disorders are rampant in show biz. Sometimes I hug an actress on my show and it's like I'm hugging skin and bone. Just remind your daughter that she's beautiful and that she's worthy and that there is a place in the acting world for everyone. If you seriously suspect an eating disorder, you can reach out to a support group that can help you intervene. Don't ignore it if your mama-radar is sensing there is a dangerous problem here.

## HOT TOPIC

### Is It an Eating Disorder?

If you notice any of the following, don't hesitate to get help. The National Association of Anorexia Nervosa and Associated Disorders (www.anad.org) and the National Eating Disorders Association (www.nationaleatingdisorders.org) both have confidential help lines. The sooner you help a loved one, the better her chance for recovery.

According to experts, these are often red flags for an eating disorder:

- Obsession with body and/or weight
- Obsession with calories
- Dieting even when already thin
- Rapid, unexplained weight loss or weight gain
- Taking laxatives or diet pills
- Compulsive exercising
- Making excuses not to eat or avoiding situations that involve meals
- Going to the bathroom frequently
- Eating alone, at night, or in secret
- Hoarding or hiding junk food/high-calorie food

• • • • • • • • • • • • • • • • • • • • • • • • • • • • • • • • • • • • •

**I have a huge ass. I'm not talking Beyoncé or Kim Kardashian bootylicious, I'm talking too big to fit into a seat on the subway. I am not overweight, I just always had a lot of junk in the trunk. I don't know what to do about it.**

If you feel like your "huge ass" is derailing your confidence and making you uncomfortable, then I say stop suffering and do something. There are only two options here: Either accept your ass the way it is (doesn't sound like you want to do that) or get a reduction. I would not suggest surgery because that requires anesthesia, and I think people take being put under way too lightly. Look into Mesotherapy (http://www.mesotherapy.com/) or Smartlipo (http://www.juvaskin.com/smartlipo.htm). They'll take you down little by little. You won't totally lose your ass, but it will get smaller and more contoured. A few needles in your behind once a week for the next twelve weeks might do you well. But I also want to point out that lots of women would KILL to have your "ass-ets"—butt enlargements are all the buzz! But in the end (pun intended), you're the one who has to be happy.

**Since I had two kids, my boobs are hanging down to my knees. My husband wants me to get them lifted and he offered to give me plastic surgery for my fortieth birthday this year. Do you think I should?**

Your breasts have served you well. You have nourished two children and you obviously are a woman of a particular age. Your husband wants you to get them lifted, so if it's something you want to do for yourself (not just for him), then you have earned that right. No apologies, girlfriend! Since he's suggested it, maybe you can both do the research together. Find the surgeons, go to the appointments, and talk about it together as a couple. I went through it with my husband and I was grateful to have his support as well as an extra pair of ears when listening to all the medical jargon.

**I know you can understand this. I hate being tall. I'm nineteen and five eleven. I can never wear heels and I'm tired of always bending over to talk to people. And what guy wants to go out with an Amazon?**

Sister, you are preaching to the choir. When I was your age, I also hated my height. I very rarely wore high heels, and I would slouch or round my shoulders or lean on one hip to shave off a few inches. All of this stuff does nothing but wear on your self-esteem. Girl, you are not going to get any smaller. It's a short world we live in, and you've got to embrace your height. The sooner you do it, the better. Hopefully, you won't be like me—I did not own it until I was thirty-three! I would never date shorter guys and I always wore dumpy flats, which made me look like a Fashion Don't. I promise you, it's the most liberating feeling to come to terms with your height! I love sexy, four- and five-inch heels now, and I get upset when I am not the tallest woman in the room. Be proud and be happy that everyone has to look up to you!

**I am twenty-four and I have really bad teeth. Some are broken, some are crooked, but I can't afford to go to the dentist and get them fixed. I am really embarrassed to smile. What should I do?**

I am telling you right now, fix your teeth. I'm a tooth person. I spent four years in braces and I am proud of the result. When my teeth start to fail me, I will get them all pulled out and get the biggest, whitest Chiclet smile known to man. It makes me cringe when I see people with screwed-up teeth. Particularly women. How you care for your teeth reflects how you take care of the rest of your life. Bad teeth will keep you out of good jobs, and hold you back from socializing. And I hate to hear that you don't like to smile! What kind of life is that? I know dental work is expensive and not many insurers cover it. Save your money if you can, or look into dental schools or clinics that offer free or low-cost treatment.

**I am a twenty-one-year-old woman with the body of a twelve-year-old boy. Seriously. No boobs. No curves. No ass. My best friend says I should have some enhancements made, but (a) I can't really afford it, and (b) I'm terrified to go under the knife. Is there anything else you can suggest?**

First, I am going to ask you to do your best to fall in love with your body. Learn how to work it. Learn how to dress it. For instance, a wrap dress is better for your body type than a straight sheath. A wrap dress creates a waist for women with no waists. Also, you might want to go bra shopping because there are bras that will pad, pump, and push up what you have. There are even undies that can lift and pad and give you a more shapely butt. Fake it till you make it!

I am going to say no to surgery at least for another ten years, and I am going to tell you why. Surgery is very expensive, and you are too young right now to be throwing away ten thousand dollars on breast implants. You have student loans to pay back and your first apartment to move into. So unless your parents are going to pay (good luck!), then hold off for a few years. In the meantime, why don't you go for a consultation? It'll cost about two hundred dollars, depending on the surgeon you go to. Look online. Do some research. This way if you do decide to get surgery down the road, you can start to save your money sensibly right now.

**I want to have a boob job, but my mom is dead set against it. She said I should embrace what God gave me and not try to change it. She also said sluts have boob jobs. How do I convince her? I'm twenty years old and living at home (so she still calls the shots), but I hate being an A cup.**

Your mother sounds the way my mom did. Ya know what? By the time I got my boobs, I was twenty-nine and I had already saved my money up for the surgery. So I didn't need her money or her permission. Breast implants are a luxury. I know you want them bad, but you should not max out a credit card or take out a loan at the bank. When I got my breasts done, I did not tell my parents. They were living in Daytona Beach, Florida, and I went down to see them during one of my vacations. I already had my boobs and the liposuction done, and I arrived in a big sweatshirt and sweatpants and went directly to the pool. I took my clothes off right there and they saw the new me in my bathing suit. I knew they wouldn't say a word because they were sitting around the pool with their condo friends. I don't think they could speak anyway! They were in utter shock. So that's how I did it.

If you want to have a boob job one day, your mother has nothing to say about it. But you're right: While you're living at home, she's still the boss of you. And when you get your boob job, this is the one thing that I will say: Think long and hard about it. I have no regrets about doing mine, but I do wish I had gotten them a cup smaller. In person they are beautiful, glorious, and luxurious. I got them under the muscle so I don't need a bra. My headlights work fine; my husband loves them. I love their proportion to my body. But they're big, and I know that when you're an A or B cup, it's so tempting to go big or go home. Make sure you can live with the results.

**My twenty-eight-year-old sister is morbidly obese. I'm talking three-hundred-plus pounds and I think she needs to get a gastric bypass so she can look better. She tells me to mind my own business, but I know she can't be happy the way she is.**

I'm sure she's *not* happy the way she is, but she's twenty-eight years old, so mind your own business. Take it from someone who comes from a critical family. I've heard more mean and cutting comments from my bigmouthed family than I care to remember. You love your sister, and you hate to see her suffer. I get that. She probably does need surgery or a very good diet, but that's her choice and her decision. If she wants to eat herself into an early grave, as sad as it might seem, there is nothing you can do about it. I am sorry for the tough talk.

**I hate my face. I'm sixteen and I have serious acne; no matter what I use (and trust me, I have tried everything at the drugstore!), it still won't go away. Can I go to school with a bag over my head?**

Of course you can't! And I want you to understand that you are not alone. Half the sixteen-year-olds in the country are cursed with terrible acne. I am sure you're using the best over-the-counter stuff you can find. You need more than that. You need to go to a good dermatologist.

When my son was younger, he had terrible eczema and nothing I used on him would cure it. It used to be a part-time job for me. I took him to one, two, three doctors, and finally the fourth dermatologist figured it out. Listen, you and your mom, or whoever holds the insurance card in your house, need to concentrate on fixing this. At this point in your life you are old enough to do some of the legwork on your own. You can start calling around and researching good doctors in your area. Ask your regular doc to recommend someone. You need to go to a real dermatologist and get a prescription. I promise you, things will clear up!

**Three months ago I was diagnosed with breast cancer. I'm okay. I'm twenty-three and they caught it early and were able to do a lumpectomy. But I had a few rounds of chemo and I've lost most of my hair. I don't want people to pity me. I don't want to wear a wig or a hat. I just feel like such a freak when I look in the mirror. I know it will grow back eventually, but right now I am depressed. What should I do?**

I'm so sorry to hear about what happened to you, and I'm glad you're okay. I would suggest that you do some therapy so that you can talk your way through this. I would also suggest a wig. Yes, I said a wig. I am not talking about a costume wig that you go to Ricky's Costume shop and buy, but a *real* wig that will cost you a couple of *real* dollars but will really help your self-esteem. You know I wear wigs, right? My own hair is thin, and I don't love it, so wigs make me feel more glam and beautiful. There is no shame in it! I feel like it's a sexy accessory. Go to a real wig shop. I can tell you right now: I live in New Jersey and there is not a decent wig place within a fifteen-mile radius. But I make the effort to go to the city, where the good wigs are. Don't order online. You need to go into a shop and sit down and have someone walk you through the process. You need to try on. Don't bring any of your friends with you. This is not a joke. This is a tool to help you feel better about yourself. You are not a freak. You are an amazing, strong, courageous woman who has kicked breast cancer at twenty-three-years-young. I am in awe, truly.

## QUIZ: HOW YOU DOIN'? DO YOU HAVE A HEALTHY BODY IMAGE?

Are you always avoiding mirrors . . . or proudly modeling what your mama made ya? Answer these questions (honestly!) and check your answers below.

1. On the beach, my outfit of choice is:
   a. An itty-bitty bikini.
   b. A long-sleeved muumuu.
   c. A one-piece and sheer cover-up.

2. When I look in the mirror, my first reaction is:
   a. "Damn, I look *goooooood* . . ."
   b. "Who the hell is that person?"
   c. "Not bad for two kids and no sleep."

3. The last item of clothing I bought myself was:
   a. Sexy lingerie.
   b. Spanx.
   c. A flattering pair of jeans.

4. If someone asked, "What famous person do you look like?" I'd reply:
   a. Miss America.
   b. The Biggest Loser . . . before losing.
   c. The only person I like to look like is myself.

5. The thing I love most about my body is:
   a. Everything. I am one hot mama!
   b. Give me a minute . . .
   c. My smile—it comes from within.

**If you answered mostly A's:** You are body-proud and sing your praises loud! Good for you for being so confident. Just don't let your head get too big. They don't make Spanx for XL egos . . .

**If you answered mostly B's:** Someone needs to give you a body image pep talk fast! Nobody and NO BODY is perfect. So stop picking on yourself.

**If you answered mostly C's:** You have a healthy body image but like most of us (myself included), you can get down on yourself now and then. You have the right idea: Focus on what's fabulous, not the flaws.

• • • • • • • •

**No matter how much I shave, wax, or pluck my body, I'm one hairy woman and I hate it. But I give up! Maybe I should let it all hang out like the ladies in Europe. Your thoughts?**

Men in Europe don't mind their females furry. But to be perfectly honest with you, I don't love it. I don't have a lot of body hair, and I got mine professionally removed—all of it—about fifteen years ago. I went to a plastic surgeon, and because he had the type of laser machine that was good for black girls, I did it. Lasers might work for you, but it's not 100 percent. I shave maybe once a month. It's not a whole bunch of bushes and tufts anymore, maybe just a little fuzz—but I know it's there. And it's not my thing, so I make sure to upkeep. As far as you are concerned: to each her own. As long as you run into a guy who appreciates a hairy woman, you can do what you please.

**I'm too embarrassed to have sex with my boyfriend with the lights on. I feel like everything looks all lumpy and bumpy, especially when I am lying down naked. I think he thinks I'm nuts, but I like to keep the room pitch-dark. What should I do?**

Every girl's been there. Nobody is just born with bedroom confidence. It's something you have to teach yourself. And when you find it, the lights are on, the blinds are open, and you never swathe yourself in a bed sheet to go to the bathroom after sex again.

Your boyfriend obviously thinks you're hot, which is why he's your boyfriend. He obviously thinks there is something sexy about you and that's why he enjoys having sex with you. He doesn't notice the "lumps or bumps," so don't dwell on them. I will tell you what is better than a good body: confidence. Confidence is the sexiest thing in the world. Men are fairly simple creatures. They tend to believe whatever bill of goods you are trying to sell to them. So if you think your bod is so unattractive that you need to be in pitch-blackness to make love . . . well, he's gonna believe you! I suggest you invest in a dimmer switch—the softer light is flattering. Also, I don't know what you sleep on, but I like to sleep on animal-print sheets. I always feel like I look thinner when I lie on them. By all means walk across the room with supreme confidence. Roll your shoulders back, engage your core (a.k.a. hold your stomach in), and walk proudly even if you don't believe it. Keep doing it until you do. Guys are visual. They like to look at it. Let him take a gander and project how proud you are to be a womanly woman! When his eyes light up, I promise you won't want to be in the dark anymore.

## Oh, no, you didn't!

**I'm a post-op transgender female. I don't go around announcing it, if you get my drift, but I am pretty damn hot. I get a lot of guys coming on to me. I'm dating this guy now and I would like it to get more serious (i.e., have sex), but I haven't told him yet. I'm afraid he'll freak. I'm a 100 percent woman. Do I need I to tell that I wasn't this way forever?**

You need to be up front, in my opinion, even before a first date. I've seen a "new" vagina and it doesn't look like a God-given vagina. This guy needs to be filled in, and fast! This is a dangerous game to play with someone, and this is how people get hurt/killed. Look, there are a lot of men who would understand what you are and still enjoy being with you. But there are probably more men who are immature, adolescent, and insecure and would freak out. Tell him in a very mature way, in a public place, with a lot of light and outside of a car. Make sure there are people around so that if he spazzes out, they can help you. And by the way, if he doesn't freak and he's fine with it, it means you weren't his first one. Be careful, and in the future, please practice full disclosure.

## WENDY'S FINAL WORD

### Tips to Avoid Body Image Drama

- **See the big picture.** There isn't one celebrity out there—not even the ones who win "Hottest Man/Woman Alive"—who loves every single inch of his/her bod. We all wish we had a bigger/smaller this or that. Instead of picking yourself apart, look at the whole individual: who you are, what you do, who loves you, and whom you love back. That, my friend, is what matters. Not the size of your ass.

- **Wise up.** I don't need to tell you (do I?) that any photo you see on a magazine cover is airbrushed to gorgeous, glossy, no-cellulite-in-sight perfection. They're meant to sell magazines. They're meant to pull you in. Please don't look at these images and compare yourself! No one . . . I repeat, no one is a natural beauty. To look that good takes hours in the makeup and hair chair, and some pretty high-tech photo retouching. Understand you're being duped by the media—and don't buy into it.

- **Be good to your body.** Fad diets, pills, bingeing, starving . . . where will that get you? Most likely sick and stressed out . . . maybe even dead. Part of loving your body is treating it with respect. The more you do for it, the more it will do for you. Eat right, exercise, take deep breaths.

# CHAPTER 12

# STYLE DRAMA

Someone asked me the other day to describe my style and I didn't even have to think about it. The word *redundant* came out of my mouth effortlessly. Yes, my style is redundant. When I love something, I buy lots and lots of it.

Case in point: I have been wearing black leggings for as long as I can remember. I got my first pair at Bloomingdale's when I was in college. They zipped on the side and had stirrups under my feet. I used to wear them so much I would have to soak them in the sink because I couldn't get my laundry done fast enough.

Fast-forward to 2013, and I still wear black leggings just about every day. I have designer pairs that cost eight hundred dollars and Walgreens pairs that cost five dollars. I have leggings for working out; leggings for clubbing; leggings for work paired with a black turtleneck and a chic camel jacket, belted at the waist.

Way back when—when I was much larger—I would wear leggings and a size 5X men's shirt from the Rochester Big & Tall store. In that way, my style has evolved. I like to feel clothes next to my body now. I like them hugging me tight—I call it "snatched." I've paid so much for the body I have, and I work so hard to be disciplined with my eating and exercise, that I have banned big shirts from my wardrobe. I don't want any room for doubt that I might be gaining a pound or two. When I pass my reflection, I like to see my handiwork.

All that said, I do think personal style is a choice. Don't listen to what people say—you make your own fashion rules. I was once described as a walking, talking Christmas tree many years ago, and I swear I wasn't insulted. I loved it! I'm from Jersey and I love all things sparkly. My style may not be for the faint of heart, but it fits me.

Anyway, let's talk about you!

**I love my cleavage. I was born with these girls and I am proud of them! All my friends and my family wish I would keep them in check. I say there**

**Is nothing wrong with a neckline that shows off that you are all woman. What do you think?**

When I first got my implants, I was that girl. In fact, I was that girl for about five years! The lower the neckline, the better. Now I'll be honest with you: I look back at that period of my life and think, "Gosh, I was really vulgar!" I think sometimes you can have too much of a boob thing going on. You have to ask yourself: Are you being tasteful . . . or letting it all hang out? A hint of cleavage in public is fine; going practically topless is not. I know you're happy; I know you're proud. Just make sure you're being flashy, not trashy. If that's the case, I'm gonna have to agree with your peoples: perhaps you need to put them away now and then.

**My sister has no taste and I am not exaggerating. She will go to work in some crazy polka-dot dress, a yellow shirt, and platform go-go boots. She buys all her clothes from thrift shops and vintage stores. I've been with her on the bus and I know people laugh. She looks like a freaking circus clown.**

### Am I supposed to say nothing and let her go on dressing this way?

Yeah, you are. Leave her alone. I have a very conservative older sister and some of the things I wear off the show embarrass the hell out of her. Guess what? Her opinion doesn't count nor does anyone else's. The only opinions I care about are my husband's and my son's. And they know better than to open their mouths if they know what's good for them!

People who dress like your sister are usually very creative types. If she hasn't gotten fired from her job, then her employer is probably fine with her flamboyant fashion. Personally speaking, I believe in freedom of expression, and I don't think you should tell someone how she should dress. I know you're trying to protect her from people laughing at her or being cruel, but let her make her own choices and fight her own battles. She's a colorful character, and that's something to be applauded. That's the only way I want to see you lending a hand.

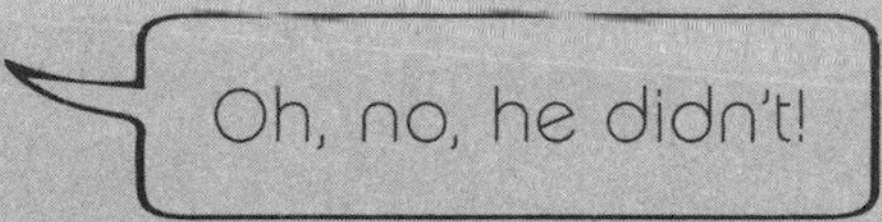


**My husband dresses like a slob! He's always in dirty jeans and old T-shirts. When we first met ten years ago, he was in an office job, and he wore nice suits and ties. Now he's working construction and he says he doesn't need to be fancy, but does this mean he needs to be a pig?**

FYI, I find construction workers very, very sexy, but I understand what you are saying. This is what you're going to do—and I want you to pay close attention. Your man is going to get organized and get himself two wardrobes. Or better yet, you're going to help him do all of the above. Wardrobe 1 is the dirty-ass stuff that he wears to the construction site. Wardrobe 2 is the stuff he wears around you. He doesn't need to look like he stepped out of GQ, but for God's sake, at least be clean, fresh, and unwrinkled. Since you are the one complaining, I am counting on you being the one to help fix this.

Buy him a pair of new jeans and a nice polo shirt. Treat him to a little bottle of cologne so he smells nice. Tell him you'd love to see him this way, and when he does clean up, run your hands through his hair and show your appreciation (and we know how men like us to show appreciation). He'll get the point.

**My boyfriend bought me a leather jacket. It was a really nice gesture and expensive, but I don't wear leather or fur. Since I am vegetarian, I thought that he would know that. Should I tell him and risk hurting his feelings or just bury it in the back of the closet?**

You should tell him—and please don't blame him for not knowing. Just because you are a vegetarian does not mean that you don't wear leather. He meant well. You don't want to be hiding the jacket from him. At some point, he's gonna wonder where it went to. Be loving and kind and don't be dogmatic about it. Go and return it together and get something that you do like. He'll appreciate your honesty and, next time, be smarter with his gift giving.

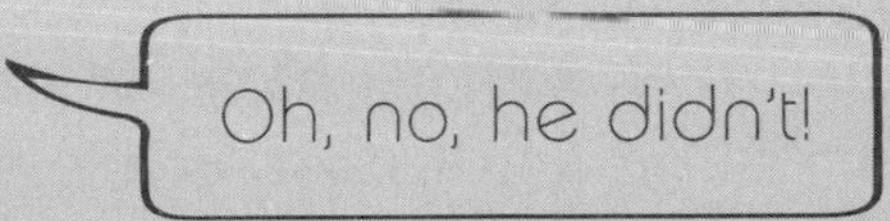


**I got this really cute cropped haircut for my twenty-first birthday and my boyfriend freaked. He said he loved my waist-long hair and that I've ruined myself. I know it's a big change, but do I need to ask his permission to change my hairstyle?**

You do not need his permission, and I hate the way he is talking to you. He said you "ruined yourself." Excuse me? So he prefers long hair. Does that mean that you have to have it all Rapunzel-like down to your waist? No! How dare he? Hair grows back, but you can't take back hurt feelings. I don't like anyone messing with my looks or telling me what to do. I've had enough boyfriends like that, and it's the reason none of them are my husband. I say cut him out of your life, girlfriend. You need a new dude along with your do.

**My sixteen-year-old daughter came home last week with her nose pierced. I wanted to kill her. How could she do this to her beautiful face? She says all the girls are doing it and I'm old-fashioned. Would you let your kid get a piercing?**

I told my son he could get his ear pierced when he was in high school, and no tattoo until college. These are my rules, and you have yours. But you know that sixteen-year-olds do sneaky things like this—and it may be because all of her friends are doing it. Welcome to the times in which we live.

The damage is done, so all you can do is prevent future piercings. Make sure she understands that while she is under your roof, your rules apply. Sit her down and set some parameters on what she will and won't do now.

I know from experience with friends that kids who have eyebrow, nose, and tongue piercings eventually tire of them. The holes close up, and your beautiful girl will go back to having her innocent face. Let's just pray she's going through a phase—and I hope that nose ring is tiny and not a bull ring! If it is . . . I'd kill her, too!

**This guy I am dating is a tattoo artist and asked if he could do some body art on me. I'm not a prude. I know it can be cool, but I am just not sure that tattoos are my style. I work at an elementary school and I dress pretty conservatively. How do I handle it?**

You handle it like you just told me. Tell him how you feel and why you feel that way. Tattoos aren't for everyone. I have a tattoo and I wish I never had to get it. My tummy-tuck mark went from hipbone to hipbone because I had a lot of loose skin. The scar healed beautifully, but you could see the line. I was putting Dermablend on every time I wore a bikini. So one day, about nine years ago, I had this midlife crisis and made my husband go with me to a tattoo parlor. I took a few belts of Jack Daniel's and got this vine and a star inked right where the line was. It's pretty stupid, but it serves its purpose. No more Dermablend.

As for you, you're dating this guy. Respect him and respect what he does for a living. Ask that he do the same for you. I find it perfectly sensible to think about your career and your lifestyle before putting any ink on your body. If you are going to get a tattoo, get something cute that you can hide (not his initials!). But don't let him push you into it. I am not a tattoo person and I will tell that to anyone who will listen. I think women on the red carpet with tattoos showing on the arms or backs in their evening gowns look ridiculous. If you feel the same, then that's your right.

**I'm Goth and my parents think it's gross. I've been dressing this way since I was fourteen, and I'm now eighteen. They are on my case to grow up and stop wearing dark makeup and dyeing my hair black. They say I won't get a job unless I do. What do you say? Shouldn't I be free to be me?**

You have about thirty more seconds to be free to be you before I agree with your parents. And I mean that. You know I've said that I don't like people messing with my personal style, and I don't like to mess with other people's style. But come on, let's be practical. Your parents are right: Nobody's going to hire you wearing black nail polish and Goth makeup. You might be the happiest person on the planet, but who can tell under all that darkness? You're going to have trouble getting a job and trouble getting a man. Are you okay with that? Being Goth is limiting your connection to the rest of society. So here is my advice: Save your look for special times, like when you go out at night or when you're with friends who are accepting. During the day you need to straighten up and fly right.

## QUIZ: HOW YOU DOIN'? WHAT'S YOUR STYLE PERSONALITY?

Are you a hoochie mama . . . a haute couture queen . . . or somewhere in between? If you're not sure, then answer the following and check your answers below.

1. The three words I would use to describe my look are:
   a. "T and A."
   b. "Professional, polished, classic."
   c. "Edgy, artsy, fun."

2. My outfit is never complete without:
   a. Four-inch stilettos.
   b. Pearl earrings.
   c. Nail art.

3. My style icon is:
   a. Snooki.
   b. Michelle Obama.
   c. Nicki Minaj.

4. If I'm going to a party, I'll wear:
   a. No underwear.
   b. A cocktail dress.
   c. Something that gets everyone's attention.

5. Most of my clothes are:
   a. See-through.
   b. Basic black.
   c. Neon.

**If you answered mostly A's:** YOU'RE FLASHY. I am being polite here, because I think you sometimes overdo it and cross the borderline into trashy. I am someone who loves to feel sexy and confident—so I get what you're going for. But there are ways to go about it, and commando is not one I'd recommend. Tone it down a tad. You want to look like a hot babe . . . not a hooker.

**If you answered mostly B's:** YOU'RE CLASSY. No one would ever accuse you of not looking put together. Just make sure your attempts to dress "appropriate" don't translate into "drab and boring." It's okay to accessorize and spice things up a little, especially when you go out at night. Save the conservative attire for day and let your hair down a little.

**If you answered mostly C's:** YOU'RE ARSTY. I know a lot of music and entertainment people that fall into this style type. You like to push the envelope with your outfits, and big and bold are your mottoes. Honey, this Jersey Girl salutes you. Have fun with your fashion, just make sure it doesn't set tongues wagging at work. What I wear on TV in front of millions of viewers is not necessarily what I would put on to go clubbing. Get my drift?

• • • • • • • •

**I noticed this woman I work with wears the same clothes every day. I don't think she has a lot of money, but they are looking pretty worn and I feel bad for her. Should I offer to loan her some of mine or give her a gift card to Gap?**

That is very generous of you, and there is a way you can do this so she doesn't feel that her dignity has been shredded. I'd suggest giving her a gift card to a store where she can get cheap, cheerful new clothes. Try to make it for an occasion like her birthday or a holiday, or even a thank-you for a job well done. Be delicate and tactful. Don't mention that you notice she has nothing to wear. Don't act like you pity her. I'd give her a twenty-five or fifty-dollar gift card to Target, Walmart, Kohl's, or Kmart. These are all great stores where she can get a lot more bang for the buck.

**This guy I really like invited me to a wedding. What do I wear? I don't have any money to buy new clothes and most of the clothes in my closet are casual. I can't even borrow because I am a big girl and none of my friends are my size.**

And why would you think you can't find any clothes that cost near-nothing just because you are a big girl? Scout out Target or Walmart for something simple like a little black dress or a long, flowy maxi. If you don't have time to hit the racks, shop online. I love Torrid (www.torrid.com) for their hip and modern looks. Dress up that dress with a pretty scarf or shawl, some dramatic costume jewelry, and heels. (Make sure they're not scuffed.) Make sure your makeup, nails, and hair are perfection. Cinderella's fairy godmother couldn't have done better! So get your butt to that wedding and have a great time.

**I am a bag whore. I can't stop buying purses, totes, and clutches. I love them, and I wear a different one every day. I have about a hundred in my closet. My husband says it's**

**a disease. I say it's my style and my prerogative; I work and it's how I want to spend my money. Wendy, what do you say?**

I love bags, too. You know why I? Because bags never let you down. As women we get fat, we get thin, we get old, but our bags are always our friends. And I have a world-class collection of handbags—all different shapes, designs, and colors. They call to me. My husband, like yours, doesn't think I need so many. That's because men, for the most part, carry only one bag, and that's to stuff their smelly gym clothes in or to tote around papers and a laptop. So here's what I say on the subject: If you can pay for your own things, you don't need to ask your spouse's permission to splurge now and then. Hopefully your purses aren't so pricey that they are digging into the family income. If they're not, then stop showing your hubby every one you bring through the door. Let it be our little secret.

## HOT TOPIC
### When Should You Spend on a Trend?

In today . . . out tomorrow. Before you lay out your hard-earned cash on the latest fad (and kick yourself later)—consider:

- **Will it last?** No one has a crystal ball that can tell you if a trend is fleeting or here to stay. You have to use your head. Is this an item that has longevity? Can I pair it with lots of things in my closet? Can I wear it several different ways (i.e., a scarf tied around my neck, my waist, my purse?). Can it be altered (shortened/recycled) into a new look when this one phases out? Could the cut/color be considered classic? Hint: If it's neon yellow, it's probably not going to be around for long.

- **Can you pull it off?** You need to be brutally honest with yourself. Just because Rihanna is rockin' it, doesn't mean it will look good on you. I say try anything on once, but if you're not feeling it, leave it on the rack.

- **Is this an impulse purchase?** I love a bargain. When I see something marked down or with a big 50-percent-off sign hanging over it in the store window, I drool like Pavlov's dog. But I urge you to be wise with your buys. If you see something trendy that's on sale, don't just snatch it up. When items get reduced in price, it's usually for a good reason—i.e., they're about to become yesterday's news. Unless you truly need it/want it, keep on walking.

..................................

**I hate my husband's old college sweatshirt, so I tossed it in the incinerator not thinking he'd notice. He noticed. Should I fess up or play dumb?**

Your husband and I have a lot in common. There are certain things that I just cannot throw out for sentimental reasons. Don't be grossed out, but I kept my son's belly button that fell off when he was a baby in our freezer for twelve years. I also have an old college sweatshirt, and a couple of things from high school that I would absolutely die if someone incinerated. They are pieces of nostalgia; they are pieces of me. Do not tell your husband what you did. It was insensitive—so please don't fess up to it. He will never forgive you. Play dumb and pray he has a spare somewhere.

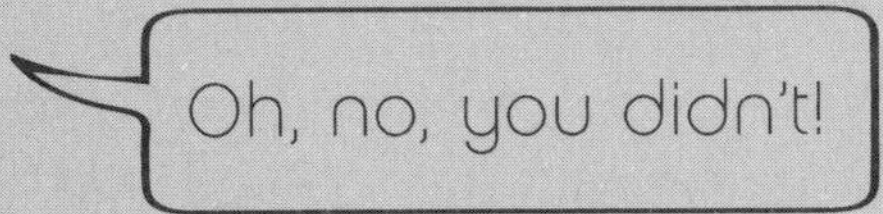


**My boss gave me an expensive pair of gold earrings for my birthday. They weren't my style, so I returned them to the department store and bought myself an iTouch. She asked why I never wear them. Now what?**

If were you, I would have kept the earrings. Sorry, they might not be your style, but it wouldn't have killed you to keep them in your desk drawer and put them on every now and then. It's important to stay on your boss's good side, and something like this could really make her sour on you. For anyone else in your life, I would say be honest and tell them the truth. But with someone you work for, you're going to have to fib to save face. Tell her you lent them to your mother. Tell her she just flipped over them and begged you to let her borrow them.

Don't tell her you lost them, because that shows you're irresponsible. If you have the money—or you can return the iTouch—I'd encourage you to purchase them back and wear them every few weeks. Your boss spent a pretty penny on you; keeping them and wearing them is the politically correct thing to do.

Oh, no, you didn't!

**I borrowed my sister's diamond studs to wear to a wedding and I lost one. I can't afford to replace it, so I went and got a pair of CZs that looked the same and gave them to her. She hasn't figured it out yet. Should I tell her?**

I wouldn't. If she can't tell the difference, consider yourself blessed. Hold on to the real stud and pray she doesn't ever need to get them appraised. I have real jewelry and fake jewelry, and I swear, sometimes I can't tell them apart. If you feel very guilty, then save your money and, one day, buy her a matching diamond stud and swap them out for the fakes. But until then, unless you want a sister who never speaks to you or trusts you again, keep your lips zipped.

## WENDY'S FINAL WORD

### How to Avoid Style Drama

Dare to wear whatever you like—it's your personal choice. Just keep in mind:

- **Don't get in debt.** Yes, you want to look good, but you don't want to max out your credit cards in the process. Keep an eye on your spending and set a reasonable budget for monthly purchases.

- **Runways are not reality.** Just because you see something in a magazine or on the red carpet, doesn't mean it belongs on you. Learn to interpret trends to fit your look and your lifestyle.

- **Weed out your wardrobe.** If more than half your clothing is from the eighties, I'm recommending an extreme style makeover.

- **Loosen up on labels.** If your motto is "Prada or Nada," you're too hooked on designer duds. It's okay to splurge now and then on a status item, but if all your clothes have someone else's name stitched in them, it's time to rethink.

## CHAPTER 13

# MONEY DRAMA

I am very comfortable talking about money. Most people aren't, but I have no problem going up to someone and saying, "OMG! I love your bag. How much was it?" I like to know what things cost, and I don't mind discussing numbers. I think it's because I was financially oblivious for so long.

When I was growing up, I always assumed there was a money tree growing in the backyard. My mother had the diamonds and the furs and the Lincoln Continental and the BMW 735i. We had a beautiful house on an acre and a housekeeper. I had more Calvin, Gloria Vanderbilt, and Izod than I knew what to do with. My parents never talked about our finances in front of me, so I grew up blissfully ignorant.

As a result, I was a spender for years and the money ran out quickly. When I was twenty-seven, I was not thinking of putting money in the bank for my golden years. Now, pushing fifty, I think about it *a lot*. Now I'm a saver. There is nobody to fund my retirement but me, and I did not marry rich. Instead of buying a fancy car, I'd rather put money away for my son's college fund. That's what age does to you: It makes you more frugal! When I became an adult, and my parents weren't paying my way anymore, I was suddenly confronted with how much everything costs. I didn't know how to handle it, and it took time for me to understand financial responsibility. I went through a lot of lean years.

Today, I thank God I have a job on TV and a steady paycheck and I can afford to give my son a good life. Do I allow myself to splurge now and then? You're damn right! Most recently on this sparkly purple bag I saw in the Louis Vuitton store in Vegas. I hesitated; I thought it was ridiculously expensive. But my husband talked me into it. "Wendy, do it," he told me. "You work really hard. You deserve it." So six thousand dollars later, it was on the plane coming home with us.

Despite my occasional designer-bag binge, I've learned that money should be respected. It's not something you should hand over easily, not to a friend, not to a store, not to your kid who says he needs yet another pair of $150 sneakers. I think long and hard before I shell out. I put away quite a bit before I treat myself. I balance my checkbook and I make sure my bills are paid on time. And I'm teaching my son to do the same. We talk money in my home. Little Kevin understands that nothing is simply handed to you. He has a bank account and he works for every cent he's given. When he buys something he's been saving up for, he's proud.

I know money is the cause of a lot of drama in people's lives. Whether you have more or less, it ignites fires. So treat it with caution . . . you're playing with matches.

**I am thirty years old and broke. I am living paycheck to paycheck, just trying to pay my rent. I don't know how to dig myself out of this hole I am in. Help!**

Even though you need most of what you make to live on, you have to start saving. That is the only way out. Stop going to Starbucks and paying seven dollars for a coffee. Make your coffee at home. You need to assess your life and decide what can stay and what needs to go. Can you find a cheaper place to live? Sell your car and take public transportation? Give up the fancy haircuts and mani/pedis, and DIY instead? You hear what I'm saying: You need to pare it down. I was you many years ago. We all go through it when we're trying to establish ourselves. If you can sock away even five dollars a week, it will make a difference. Every cent you put into your nest egg will help it grow.

## HOT TOPIC
### Fast Cash!

Looking to wind up with a little extra money in your pocket at the end of the month? Why not . . .

- **Withdraw only from your bank ATM.** Unless it's an emergency, don't take cash from any ATM that charges a fee. You may be paying as much as three dollars every time you withdraw.

- **Turn a hobby or talent into a business.** Sell your wares on Etsy or eBay to earn extra cash. Or look through your attic or closets for "antiques" that some collector might want. I know one woman who sold her old Barbie dolls for five hundred dollars!

- **Buy bulk with a buddy.** Hit Costco and split a case of whatever you need with a friend.

- **Freeze leftovers and reuse scraps.** If the recipe calls for a half an onion or one garlic clove, don't toss the rest away. Save for another day.

- **Swap, don't shop.** Ask friends to come over and bring clothes and accessories they no longer love or wear. You all trade and walk away with a new wardrobe without spending a dime.

- **Bring lunch.** If you spend just five dollars a day on fast food, it adds up to hundreds a year. Brown-bag it once or twice a week and put that ten bucks in your piggy bank.

- **Break a bad habit.** Smoking and drinking may be costing you thousands of dollars a year. Ditch your vice, and your insurance premiums and medical bills will also go down. Plus you'll live longer, so you can enjoy what you socked away.

**My twenty-five-year-old best friend just inherited a lot of money. She's going crazy spending it: new car, new clothes, new furniture, fancy restaurants. I told her to slow down and put some away. Should I mind my own business? If I got a windfall like that, I would at least put some in the bank. I think she is being reckless and stupid.**

You can't tell her how to spend her money. The second you do, she's going to tell you you're jealous and the friendship will be over. Right now she's not seeing tomorrow. She's hit the jackpot and that's all she's focused on. She wants to have fun, not open an IRA. I get it; I was the same way. I hope she wises up and matures before she blows everything she has. You can try to broach the subject lightly: "Girlfriend, I love all the stuff that you are getting, but I hope you're saving some, too . . ." Otherwise, just keep your mouth shut and resist the urge to lecture. And look on the bright side: She's going to need a partner to go to those fancy restaurants. She's going to need a wingman in that expensive car of hers. If she insists on being reckless, you might as well go along for the ride.

**My husband and I are going through some rough times. He lost his job and I make minimum. My grandma left me a lot of jewelry when she passed away. He thinks I should sell it. It's the only thing I have left to remember her by!**

I know it's sentimental, but your grandmother is looking down on you and she understands. Keep one piece to remember her by—your favorite one—and sell the rest. Your husband doesn't seem like some Svengali who is making you sell granny's jewels. He's out of work and you need the money. If this will keep your heads above water for a while, then by all means, don't think twice. Sell it.

**I asked my boss for a raise and she flat-out said no. I know she's given other people in my division raises, but I've noticed that they are all married with families. Am I supposed to make less because I am single?**

It's not right or fair, but silently it's done all the time. A lot of companies discriminate against single ladies.

I've got a friend who is the same age as me who's not married and has no children, and she gets stuck with the shitty hours and the shitty vacation time. Why? Because the married coworkers get Christmas Eve, Easter, etc. to spend with their families.

Your boss expects you to be married to your job—that's pretty clear—yet she doesn't want to compensate you for it. If you feel you've earned it, then ask again at a later time. You're going to get that raise next year or else!

## HOT TOPIC

### Should You Take Out a Loan?

Sometimes we find ourselves in a financial crisis and a quick fix sounds *so* good. People ask me a lot if they should take out loans. I believe you don't buy anything you can't pay for—but that's just me. Like I said, I've grown out of my overspending phase, and now I'm all about saving. But having been financially irresponsible, I do understand that it's very stressful to feel tapped out. And sometimes, ya gotta do what ya gotta do. Borrowing is way better than robbing a bank. I'm no Suze Orman, but I would consider this before taking out a loan:

- **Do you need the money *right* now?** If it's a purchase (new car, new house, new anything), can you postpone it till you have some more cash saved up? Do you really need that vacation . . . or could it wait a few months or years?

- **Can you pay it back?** Be honest. Can you make the monthly payments? Have the entire sum and interest paid off in a year? If the answer is no, then I say no to borrowing.

- **Is this loan a good investment?** Are you using it to pay for college or law school now? Will it help your ability to earn money?

- **Are you forgetting about the future?** By dipping into your nest egg or your retirement fund, you get a quick infusion of cash . . . but at what cost? Do you have enough time to replace that money so you'll be safe and secure in your old age? I don't know about you, but I don't want to be broke and old. I want to be sitting in my rocking chair, counting my cash!

**My daughter thinks college is a waste of money and won't take out a student loan to pay for it. I was so happy when she was accepted; now I feel horrible. I wish we had saved more to send her, but we didn't. What can I do? Is it too late?**

If she thinks it's a waste of money, then you can't force her. If her heart isn't in it, she'll be the girl who flunks out freshman year. I come from a family of college graduates, including my mom and dad. College was not something I questioned whether or not I was going to do. I knew I owed my parents four years. My son will owe me and his father the same thing. Once he graduates from high school, he's got to go to a four-year university. Then he can go off and live his life.

That said, college is not for everyone. What does your daughter want to do? Does she want to go to a trade school? Join the army? Travel the world? What does she want to do with her life? She can't just sit around your house sponging off of you. Have the talk. Be open-minded and try and guide her. And don't give up: She may not want to go to college right away, but it's never too late. After a little soul-searching, she might have a change of heart.

## Oh, no, you didn't!

**I got kicked out of my apartment by my roommate because I couldn't cover my share of the rent. I just can't get my act together when it comes to money. I always think I have enough and then the checks bounce. Help!**

What part of 1 + 1 = 2 do you not understand? I am sorry for being upset with you, but you have really screwed up. Your roommate kicked you out and I hope she changed the locks, too. Nobody has time for you and your irresponsibility. You don't have to be wealthy to develop a relationship with money. If you know all you have in the bank is $100, don't write a check for $125. Cut up your ATM card if you are constantly withdrawing and not keeping track of the cash that comes out.

You're asking for my help, so I'm going to tell you what to do. Starting right now, carve out an hour once a week to go over your finances. Check your balances online so there are no more surprises. How much have you saved? What are your expenses and where will it leave you by the end of the month after you've taken care of them? Don't let yourself get caught with your pants down. Every time you bounce a check, your bank charges you a whopping fee—usually about thirty-five dollars. You should always know how much you have coming in and going out. If you're old enough to have your own apartment, then you're old enough to balance your checkbook. Shame on you! Get your act together!

**My mom is loaded. She married a guy (her third husband!) who makes millions every year and she's having a great time spending it. My husband and I don't have a pot to piss in. Shouldn't she share with us?**

No. Why should she share with you? You're grown enough to get married, so now get out there and make your way. Your mother's millionaire man sounds fabulous, but that is *her* fabulous. He is not your father. He owes you nothing. What I want to know is this: Are you jealous of your mother's windfall, or are you truly desperate to keep afloat financially? Are you in danger of losing your home? Getting sued by bill collectors? That's another case. If you have a good relationship with your mom, you could confide in her and ask for some "squeezin's" to tide you over. That's what we called a couple of dollars growing up in the Williams house. I wouldn't involve your husband. And if she says no, then it's no. There is truly no obligation on her part to save your ass.

**My husband insists that we combine all of our finances now that we're married. That's great for him—he has nothing saved. But I've worked hard in my teaching career to put a decent amount of money aside. Am I being horrible in saying I want separate bank accounts?**

In my opinion, not all money in marriages should be commingled. I think that's very *Ozzie and Harriet,* very old school. These days, a lot of us modern girls don't get married until our careers are established and we're making money. I believe in "I have what I have and you have what you have." You can put some of your money into a joint account with him, and he can do the same: a yours, mine, and ours approach. Your husband may start jumping up and down like a gorilla and say, "Why would you want to keep money from me?" A lot of guys can't deal with that. Fortunately, I'm not married to one of those.

You're sharing your lives, your home, your bed, but you simply want a bank account that is all yours to save and spend as you see fit. Sit down, discuss your savings goals together, discuss how you will handle the monthly expenses. Part of being newlyweds is figuring these things out. But if you are asking my opinion . . . I think this is one issue you have to stand your ground on. You earned your money and you have earned the right to keep some of it all to yourself.

## QUIZ: HOW YOU DOIN'? WHAT'S YOUR DOLLARS AND SENSE?

Do you let yourself get into debt up to your eyeballs? Or do you sock away every cent? Take this quiz to figure out your saving/spending style:

1. SCENARIO 1: Your nineteen-year-old daughter announces (surprise!) she's engaged! She wants a big wedding and an elaborate honeymoon. You:
   a. Take out a second mortgage on the house and sell the gold fillings in your teeth so she can have carte blanche.
   b. Explain that you will contribute as much as you can, but she and her fiancé and his family will also have to pay up.
   c. Hide all your money and credit cards under the mattress—she's on her own!

2. SCENARIO 2: You win $500,000 in the Lotto. You:
   a. Book a trip around the world and buy that hot sports car you've always dreamed of.
   b. Put the bulk of the money in a 529 plan to save for your kids' college and treat the family to a fun vacation.
   c. Take out a long-term CD so you won't be able to touch it.

3. SCENARIO 3: Your BFF tells you she's heard about an amazing "can't lose" investment opportunity. You:

   a. Write her a big check—you're eager to have your money triple in a month!
   b. Ask for more info: How much would you need to invest and how risky is it?
   c. Sever all contact with so-called BFF. Anyone who wants your money is no friend of yours.

4. SCENARIO 4: Your child's school calls asking for a donation for a new library. You:

   a. Cover the cost and ask for the library to be named in your honor.
   b. Offer to make a small donation that you can afford.
   c. Reply, "Thanks, but I think reading is overrated."

5. SCENARIO 5: Your roof springs a leak and needs repair. You:

   a. Sell the dump fast and move somewhere better.
   b. Get an estimate on the cost and discuss with your spouse how you will pay for it.
   c. Put a few buckets in the bedroom—what's a few drips?

**If you answered mostly A's:** YOU'RE A BUY-TODAY, PAY-TOMORROW GIRL. You like to live on the edge financially and spend impulsively. Is it any wonder your credit cards are all maxed out? Honey, this isn't Monopoly. All those charges you are racking up are real. I want you to take a deep breath and think before you buy. Get a financial planner or at the very least put a lock on your checkbook. Please, please, please!

**If you answered mostly B's:** YOU'RE A SMART SPENDER. You don't live beyond your means, and you consider all the possible outcomes before you make an investment or dig into your purse. You save but you also allow yourself a treat now and then. Kudos to you for learning to be a grown-up.

**If you answered mostly C's:** YOU'RE A MISER. Seriously: Scrooge has got nothin' on you, girlfriend. Why so tight with your money? That twenty-dollar bill won't cry if you break it! There's a lot of merit in saving, but you're not tightening the purse strings—you're strangling them. Consider creating a little "mad money" fund that allows you to enjoy life as well as plan for your future.

• • • • • • • •

## WENDY'S FINAL WORD

### How to Avoid Money Drama

Money is not the root of all evil . . . especially if you do the following:

- **Understand it.** Don't just dump all financial dealings on your parents, your spouse, your roommate. You need to know how to pay a bill, balance your checkbook, how much interest is being charged on each of your credit cards. Educate yourself by reading books, articles, and asking questions. That nice employee in the bank will be glad to explain (and might be a hottie!).

- **Don't be a sucker.** Salespeople are paid to sell . . . which means they want you to buy. If you can't afford what they're hawking, than walk away. No impulsive purchases; no buying what you can't immediately pay for. I'd actually recommend making purchases only in cash. You can't have credit-card debt if you don't have credit cards.

- **Save.** Simple: Put money, even if it's only the spare change in your pocket, away every day. It adds up, and you'll soon find you have a little nest egg.

- **Set a budget.** This is basically a financial wish list. This is what I want/need and this is how much I have in my pocket, liquid, to get it. Stick to it. No fudging the figures or ignoring the bottom line.

*Dear Reader:*

*I hope that you enjoyed reading this book. If you didn't agree with me on every topic, please don't hate me! I know I've got some pretty strong opinions, and they might not be yours. I'm just a woman from New Jersey with a few life lessons under her belt.*

*You've written the letters, and I've answered the questions. I've responded honestly and from my heart. This book has taken me through a range of emotions that I can't even fully express to you. I have laughed and I have cried, and through it all, I've tried to give you the very best advice I can muster. I turned off the TV, shut the doors to my mom cave, and clutched my Kleenex box. The process was overwhelming but also an overwhelming joy.*

*There were several times I called my mom. She's almost eighty, so I figure she's been around the block a little more than I have. She's one of the old cool hip dolls that we thank God for. "Shirley," I'd say (I call my mom, Shirley), "you won't believe this letter." And then we'd talk it over, weighing the pros and the cons of every option. Everyone needs a second opinion sometimes. That's why you've come to me with your questions, right? You probably know exactly what to do . . . you just need someone to say it out loud. Or in my case . . . in print.*

*I've always known that every answer to every question we have in our lives lies within. Just like the Magic 8 Ball says. You are smarter than you know, dear heart. You can solve your own problems. Clear the clutter out of your life and stop listening to your friends and even me. Only you know what's best for you. There, I've said it. If I was standing next to you, I'd give you a kick in the ass. If there is drama in your life, then you know why, and you know how to get rid of it. Maybe the choice is a hard one. No one promised you an easy ride. But do it. Act on your instinct. Fix what's broken. Find what's missing.*

*One day, you'll be older and wiser and you'll look back on my advice and say, "You know, I thought that Wendy chick was nuts back then. Now I kinda get it." You will get it. One day it will all click. I am not the same person I was thirty years ago. The mistakes I made then I would not make now. My opinions have changed, and I am sure they'll continue to change. Isn't it a woman's prerogative to change her mind? Fool me once, shame on you. Fool me twice, shame on me! And I can look back now and see where I went wrong. Hopefully, I'll save you some time and aggravation.*

*So one last word of advice from ol' Wendy: Drama rears its ugly head for a reason. It's to teach us what we want and don't want in our lives. It's to make us move forward in a direction that we're meant to take, maybe not now, maybe not tomorrow, but eventually. It shows us that we're all human; we all make mistakes. I have learned that you can never change people, only the way you react to them. So if your sister, or mother, or boss, or best friend or man is driving you up the walls, what are you going to do about it? Are you going to wait for them to stop (good luck!), or are you going to do something?*

*Just know that no matter how hard the choice is that you have to make, I'm on your side. Thanks for sharing with me and for letting me share with you.*

# ACKNOWLEDGMENTS

Thank you to my writing partner, Sheryl Berk, and to my business partner, Jill Ramsey, for making this process painless. Thank you to my understanding staff. And most of all, thanks to my adoring *Wendy* watchers around the world for welcoming me into your private lives and for allowing me to help with your important personal issues.

**Keep Reading for a Preview of**
**Wendy Williams's Next Release**
**HOLD ME IN CONTEMPT**
**Coming in April 2014**

The worst thing about being a black lawyer is that everyone you know thinks you're *their* lawyer and they can call you about anything at any time. And while I'm sure that happens to all lawyers—white, yellow, brown, and beige—because I'm black it's almost a guarantee that whatever my people need me for at whatever time is likely so ghetto and/or hood there's simply no way I can tack my signature to anything having to do with the situation. Now, that may sound uppity to some black folks and flat-out hateful to others, but I bet not one black lawyer considering my statement will disagree. And that's because it's the truth.

Case in point: my cousin Tyree got pulled over last month for speeding on the FDR Drive. Doesn't sound too bad. . . . Add, though, that it was four o'clock in the morning, Tyree is a convicted felon with hard-time muscles and shady gang prison tattoos from wrists to neck, he was high on crystal meth and naked, and his car was packed with frozen hot dogs he'd stolen from Gray's Papaya. (In case anyone is wondering: I can't even try to make this crap up. It was on the news.) Now, this little string of drama is totally in Tyree's range of ridiculousness, so no one should judge. But according to the actual police report, when officers in squad cars and helicopters had their bright lights and guns pointed at his muscly black body in the dead of night on one of the busiest highways in New York City, this fool stepped out of the car and demanded that someone call his "fucking lawyer Kimberly Kind."

This was repeated more than fifty times before they wrestled his silly ass to the ground and got him into one of the police cars.

*Did I mention that this was in the actual police report? . . . And on the news?*

I should've stayed my black behind in bed because I was due in court in the morning, but you can't say no to your aunt Sissy when she calls you wailing in the middle of the night to go get her "baby boy" out of jail. No matter what I had going on, at that moment I was expected to make some kind of magic happen . . . or I'd face a jury of my peers who'd find me guilty of "acting funny" or worse "forgetting where I came from." And that's a whole other conversation.

Now, I knew whatever my twin brother had in mind when he called this morning asking me out to brunch wasn't too far from Tyree's antics on the FDR. As my grandmother used to say, Tyree and Kent were cut from the same cloth and though my brother had less strikes behind his name, the last time he'd called at six A.M, it was because he'd gotten caught selling black market Newports at Rucker Park.

Still, I agreed to meet him in Hell's Kitchen at my favorite Sunday brunch spot, 44 & X. He was paying, so it was all good.

I showed up an hour late, but he wasn't there, so I chose a table out on the street where I could see the sun and enjoy the loud white noise of a city that had no tolerance for standing still. I ordered a mimosa, sat back and tried to think of something lovely but a huge black fly kept buzzing in my ear.

When Kent finally pulled up on his big black motorcycle the engine roared so loudly that everyone seated at the sidewalk tables turned to see what was going on. He slid into a slender space right in front of the door and hopped off the motorcycle like someone was about to ask for his autograph.

Kent was born less than two minutes after me, but thank God we looked nothing alike. My "baby brother" was always the biggest man in any room (save when Tyree and his prison muscles were out on bail). He'd been 6'7", 290 pounds and solid since we were in high school. While he was my father's only son, when he took on our father's nickname "Mook," folks in our neighborhood in Hamilton Terrace started calling Kent "Big Mook" and Daddy "Lil Mook."

"Kiki Mimi," Kent called out with his arms extended toward me as he crept over to the table where I was sitting outside of 44 & X.

He was more than an hour late for a brunch he'd invited me to, but I stood and grinned at him anyway. I let him pick me up and spin me around like we hadn't seen each other since Emancipation. More than anyone in the world, Kent always seemed to know how to make me smile. He was my little brother and big brother at the same time.

"You're late," I said after he'd hugged me half to death and we'd settled into our seats.

"Nah. I'm right on time, love. God is always on time," he responded mystically. He'd joined the Five Percent Nation when we were in high school and still referred to himself as "God."

"Well, maybe 'God' should be an hour early next time," I said.

"Don't stress me. You've been late the last few times we were supposed to meet up, so don't play," he answered as our wide-eyed white waitress bearing a gold nameplate spelling out Holly approached the table licking her lips in his direction.

"Wha chu havin' to drink?" she asked, all sexy in hipster hip-hop lingo. She had a huge wooden dagger in her ear, a thin gold ring in her nose and a tattoo of a feather on her neck. She looked like one of those Montana-bred, recent NYU grads who'd been sleeping with black men since she'd moved out of the dorms and into an overpriced studio in the new gentrified and overpriced Bed-Stuy I hated.

"What are you drinking, Kiki?" Kent pointed at the glass in front of me.

"A mimosa." I looked at him, perplexed.

"Oh, that's what I want." Kent turned to the waitress. "Hook me up with a mimoso—"

"A mimos*a*," I cut in, correcting him.

"Yeah, that shit, yo. Give me that shit," he agreed, grinning like he knew the classy order sounded odd coming from a black biker in Timbs and a crisp white T.

Hipster Holly skipped away in her Vans as I kept my skeptical eyes on Kent.

"What you looking at?" he asked.

"A mimosa? You're drinking a mimosa?"

"Yeah. That's what's up."

"Whatever, Kent," I said. "Look. What do you want?"

"Want?"

"Need? From me."

"I don't need anything. Why I gotta need something?"

"Negro, please. You're ordering mimosas when I've never seen you drink anything but Heineken. You asked me out to brunch in Hell's Kitchen when you never leave Harlem. And you're being all nice to me. You have to want something. Just say it." I sat back and looked at little bits of skin peeling off Kent's forehead. Then I noticed that he was a little darker than he'd been the last time I'd seen him at aunt Sissy's second born-again baptism. The one thing we had in common was our clear sable complexion. Sitting outside of the restaurant, Kent looked a little more mahogany. "And is that a skin tan?" I added.

"Sho is a tan!" Kent grinned and sat back too, taking his drink from the waitress.

"From where? Where you been? Virginia Beach?" It was late May and the city was heating up, but the sun wasn't nearly close enough to microwave his brown skin so neatly.

After Holly took our brunch orders with massive amounts of hatred aimed at me and desire tossed in Kent's direction, he answered my question with too much enthusiasm: "I was in Rio—Rio de Janeiro!"

"Brazil? What were you doing in Brazil?"

"A little vacay with the fellas. You know I gots to unwind. A God be putting in work and shit. Especially now that I'm one hundred percent legit. Working man's money is funny, yo."

"Humph." I frowned. "Interesting. I didn't even know you had a passport."

"Well, you don't know everything about me," he said. "Just like I don't know everything about you."

"Very true. And I'm happy about that because God only knows what kind of foolishness went down in Rio. You went with Maurice and them?"

Kent nodded with a huge smile.

"I don't even want to think about it," I added, annoyed.

"Why?" He pretended to be surprised at the disgusted look on my face.

"Because everyone knows why men go to Brazil. And in a group? You guys were probably sleeping with everything that walked by in a thong. And paying for it. Horrible. Do you know most of those women are underage? And we won't even talk about the HIV rates."

"All praises to the Creator, those hoes were bad as hell, but I swear I didn't touch not one of them," Kent revealed, holding up his hands in mock innocence.

"Double negative," I pointed out.

"What?"

"The double negative you just used means you actually slept with many prostitutes in Brazil," I explained and heard myself sounding like a complete nerd. "Look, never mind. Whatever. I'm happy you enjoyed your nasty man vacation. Cheers!" I clinked my half-empty glass with his.

"See, look at you judging a brother. Ain't even ask why I didn't sleep with none of those Mexicans."

"Brazilians. They're Brazilian," I corrected Kent, laughing at his comical oversight. He liked to play dumb, but Kent was just as smart as I was—maybe smarter—and I was sure he knew the difference between a Mexican and a Brazilian. "But I'll throw you a bone: why didn't you sleep with any of the prostitutes, Kent?"

"I fell in love." He smiled and looked off like he was starring in some Jay-Z music video on a beach with Brazilian chicks draped over both of his shoulders and a bottle of champagne in each hand.

"In love?" I actually laughed as Holly slid our plates onto the table. "You? With whom?"

"Her name is Lydia. Lydia Santiaga. I met her at the airport. As soon as we walked out, she was standing there just greeting people. Shorty was mad ill, yo."

I closed my eyes and exhaled deeply before choosing my words—my old therapist had taught me that.

"You know what, that's great," I offered. "I'm happy you fell in love with Lydia, who was randomly waiting outside of the airport to greet some random dudes she doesn't know. But now you're back home and everything is back to normal. Have you spoken to Keisha?"

"Keisha? I ain't fucking with her. Why you bringing my baby mama up?"

"Because she's *your* baby mama and you've been with her forever." I petered out ironically.

"I just told you I'm in love," he said. He leaned into the table over our food and added more softly, "I'm going to marry her."

I was about to laugh before I realized that he was dead serious. Then a wave of confusion mixed with anger and maybe a little bit of caution washed over me, leaving me silent.

"That's why I invited you to brunch," Kent went on, "to tell you I'm in love and I'm getting married. I need you, yo."

"Need me? For what?"

"It's nothing really. Small fries for my big sister. See, Lydia got into some shit, so it's going to be hard for us to get her into the country."

"Us? What? Are you kidding me? So that's why you invited me here? To get your prostitute girlfriend into the country?"

"Don't call her a prostitute," Kent demanded, raising his voice. "She ain't like that. She's a good girl. She just got into a little trouble. That's all."

"What kind of trouble?" I looked at him as crazily as he sounded.

"She has some family in the Bronx and she was here last year visiting. Five-O picked her up on Hunts Point, saying she was hoeing, but it wasn't nothing like that."

"Really?"

"Nah, yo. She was there for her cousin's bachelor party. That's all."

"So the police just randomly found her walking the street in Hunts Point, which is known for prostitution, and arrested her?" I pushed sarcastically.

"Word!" Kent confirmed, still chewing on a bite of the salmon omelet he'd ordered. "And that's why we need you to pull some strings for her. They say she can't come back to the U.S. Not even if I marry her. And you know a nigga ain't moving to Rio to be with the meda-medas for the rest of his life, so I need you to get shorty here."

"No can do," I said flatly.

"Yes you can."

"Sure can't."

"Why not? You're the assistant district attorney for New York County. I know you can pull some strings. Call in some favors. Fuck it, call the mayor!" He laughed.

"No. I don't work in immigration and I certainly don't call in favors for this kind of crap. I save that for things like Rucker Park . . . and what was that drama you got caught up in on the turnpike?"

"Oh, you're going to bring up that cracker trooper? A nigga was just taking a piss."

"On the highway," I reminded him.

"So? That's in the past." Kent sat back again, all deflated. "See I knew you'd bring that shit up. Knew you'd act funny. I thought inviting your saddity ass out to this spot would actually make you act right. But you ain't got no act right for your baby bro."

"That's a doubleneg—" I started, but stopped myself. "Act right? So I don't have any 'act right' because I don't want to get involved with you trying to marry some woman you just met?"

"Yup. That's how you act," Kent said in a way he knew would get to me. "Like you always forget what it's like out here for niggas like me. Just trying to find love and shit. Nah mean? Folks blow up and forget where they came from. Forget how they got where they at." His eyes cut me accusatorily.

For all of Kent's faults, his many shortcomings, he never failed to support me at whatever I was doing. Our parents became addicted to crack when we were in elementary school and while he was ninety-eight seconds younger than me, Kent jumped into the role of caretaker. He stopped going to school and ran errands for the drug dealers so we had something in the refrigerator and coats in the winter. And even though our father eventually went to rehab and got clean, Kent stayed on the block to pay my way through Howard University and gave me a suitcase filled with hundreds when I was accepted to Columbia Law.

"Lydia is gonna be my wife. I love her. She's everything I've wanted in a woman—soft, beautiful, nice," he said as I ate. "She ain't nothing like these chicks here."

"I'm sure she's great, but why do you have to marry her? Why get married at all? I thought you said you didn't want any more kids. What's the point?"

"That's the thing, yo. Lydia don't want any more kids either. She already has four. She don't want no more shorties." Kent smiled like this was a plus.

"I can't listen anymore. I can't even listen anymore. This crazy. Are you serious? You're a thirty-one-year-old man. There's no way you could think this is a good idea."

"See, you're judging Lydia. You don't even know her. Look, why don't you come through the crib tonight? We gonna be on Skype and shit. You'd like her," Kent said, trying to make it sound as if the idea had just come to mind, but it was obvious that it was all a part of his plan. "And you can see your father. I know you ain't been home in a minute." He still lived in his same childhood bedroom in the brownstone our grandparents left our father.

"I've been busy at work," I said. "And I can't come tonight. I'm busy."

"Too busy to meet your future sister-in-law?"

"Meet? What am I supposed to say to her?"

"Well, you ain't gonna be saying much." Kent laughed slyly.

"Why?"

"Because she don't hardly speak no English."

"What? How do you— I don't even want to know," I said. "I'm busy tonight anyway. Tamika's son has a fencing match and I promised I'd be there to support him."

"Fencing? What the fuck cuzzo have Miles doing that shit for? That tall ass nigga need to be balling. He's like six three at thirteen."

"She just wants him to try different things. Expand his range, so he's not stuck on the basketball thing," I said, realizing that Kent wasn't listening to anything I was saying.

His eyes were ogling something behind me that I knew from experience likely had a big behind and huge breasts. I turned to see what he was eyeing so I could blast him for mentally groping a woman after he'd solemnly sworn his love and devotion to Latin Lydia. But as soon as I twisted my neck I wished I'd stayed set on Kent.

Hipster Holly the waitress was seating two people I never wanted to see again in life. Two people I'd wished dead on more than one occasion. My ex-fiancé and my former roommate/best friend. Suddenly, I wanted to disintegrate into the concrete and dribble down into the sewer—well, maybe I wanted that for them. I just wanted to disappear. Poof.

"Yo, honey is bad. Ass and titties on an Asian chick?" Kent was fanaticizing in his own little world and probably had no idea he was speaking aloud. "She got a little black in her though. Skin kinda brown. She sexy as fuck."

"Whatever." I turned back to the table and struggled so hard to swallow a gob of sad spit that had gathered at the back of my throat that I was sure everyone outside of the restaurant could hear me. I could feel my enemies turn to the table and notice me. Suddenly, I was overly aware of how my black linen slacks weren't ironed, my Hebru Brantley T-shirt looked dingy and I was in worn down flip-flops—not the chic stilettos I'd purchased for the sole purpose of running into them at some point in the city. But here? Why here? 44 & X was my favorite brunch spot and everyone knew it. They knew it. The three of us had brunch here together before. I looked like a budding lesbian who couldn't get anyone but her twin brother to take her out to brunch on Sunday afternoon.

"Real recognize real. Don't act like she ain't fine." Kent laughed like I was being petty and looked at me sinking deeper into my seat. "What? What's wrong?"

"Nothing? Look, are you ready?" I asked quickly, covering my half-eaten omelet with the napkin that had been sitting on my lap.

"Ready? What? I ain't finished eating yet." He pointed down at his salmon and eggs covered in so much ketchup it made me want to vomit. "I know you ain't that jealous. She's fine but—"

"I know her." I stopped him.

"Oh, that's what's up. Hook a nigga up." Kent sounded relieved and probably completely missed how his suggestions negated everything he'd invited me to the restaurant to achieve.

"That would be impossible," I said.

"Why?"

"Well, because you're allegedly in love with someone you met like five minutes ago and about to get married—"

"I ain't married *yet*—"

"And she's . . . on a date." I felt hot tears gathering behind my eyes at that reality.

"Fuck that. Ain't no way that little nigga is hitting that shit right. I'd bag shorty in a minute." Kent laughed. "Put me in the game, coach Kim. Hook a nig—"

"Look at the man sitting at the table, Kent," I ordered, irritated. "*Look* at him."

"What?" Kent squinted for a minute and then his mouth hung open like he was looking at a dead body for the first time. "Yooooo, that's Ronald *McDonald*. Your ex—" He stopped himself and looked at me. "Oh, that's the—Asian Kim? Wait, he's fucking Asian Kim? You ain't tell me that." He looked back at her. "I thought I recognized that ass."

"I did so tell you," I said, feeling a little tear slide from the crevice of my left eye. "I told you what she did and—?"

"Oh, don't start on that shit, Kiki Mimi," Kent said, leaning toward me like a basketball coach about to pull me out of the game. "You can't let that lame nigga see you over here crying. That shit was like two years ago when ya'll called off the wedding."

"One year, two months" I blurted out.

"So. Yo, dead that. You moved on. You better than that nigga Ronald McDonald. I mean, that nigga's *real* name is Ronald McDonald. Come on. You couldn't marry that clown."

His words were supposed to build me up, but hearing the word *marry* tore me apart and a few more tears escaped my eyes. Then Kent placing his hand on my shoulder to comfort me opened the floodgates, so I jumped up from the table to rush inside of the restaurant to the bathroom before I unraveled into a mess.

I went into a stall and locked the door behind me like a monster was on my tail when really it was just my past. Ronald McDonald was a funny name, but my history with him was nothing to laugh about. I loved that man intensely and without warranty. We'd met our sophomore year at Howard. He was skinny and too smart. He was always talking about how he was going to be a lawyer when he graduated from college and how he was going to save all the poor black people of the world. I'd always been really smart, but I had no idea what I intended to do after Howard. I was the first person in my entire family to go to college and all I knew was that after I graduated I wanted to get a good job so I could go home, find my mother, and pay for her to go to a good rehab place in Malibu or someplace in Denver like all of the white celebrities did on television.

Needless to say, skinny Ronald McDonald and all of his big talk about plans and the future was more than attractive to me. I just craved his direction and soon his dream became my dream. By junior year, he was my best guy friend and after college we were going to law school together. But there was only one thing missing from our dynamic duo—one thing that kept either of us from calling each other anything but friends: both Ronald and I were virgins. Kent and his drug-dealing crew had scared all the neighborhood boys off when I was still in high school, so I hadn't so much as made out with anyone.

All of that changed one night during homecoming weekend junior year. Ronald had pledged Kappa the semester before and he was in his chapter's step show. I got there early with my girls and sat in the front row, ready to cheer him on. We were debating who'd look the hottest onstage and who'd likely drop his cane mid-performance. I mean, these were guys we'd known since our freshman year and now they'd pledged and become pseudo celebrities on campus—or so they thought.

When the Kappas hit the stage, Ronald was right in front of me. And he was moving his body in ways that just tickled the little space behind my ears. By the middle of the show, he was shirtless and working his cane so fast, beads of sweat trickled down hard abs I'd never seen. I kept thinking, What has he been doing all summer? My girls were cheering and screaming his name, but I was speechless, standing there with my arms folded over my chest and feeling something new, twitching and hot, between my thighs.

Ronald didn't drop that damn cane at all and by the time he shimmied off the stage with his frat brothers, snaking his body back and forth, I knew I was going to be waiting for him in his dorm after we finished partying that night on Georgia Avenue.

I didn't say a word to my girls. In two years on the yard, I learned that every single one of them had a big mouth and I was so afraid that if I did something with Ronald and told them, it would get out and people would call me a "Kappa set out" (coded language for "whore"). But there was nothing wrong with doing and not telling, and I knew Ronald wasn't the type of guy to go telling his frat brothers all of his business (I mean, he was a virgin, too), so once we all left the club where Ronald had been strolling with his brothers through the party before drooling freshman girls' eyes all around, I was waiting right outside his door.

He smiled and invited me in like it was any other night and we were about to have one of our "bestie" sleepovers and watch old reruns of *Martin* after smoking a little weed, but I told him not to turn on the television. I was already drunk enough to act out what I was feeling between my thighs and I jumped right on top of him on his bed while he was in the middle of a panicky retelling of his performance like I hadn't been there. I could tell he was nervous. He hadn't ever seen me like that. His hands were sweating and I could feel his heart beating into my chest as he kissed me like the Tin Man.

That's when I felt it. I was straddling him and at his middle something was swelling and hardening fast. I'd heard about "wood" and brothers getting "hard," and I knew what it was, so I just pushed my middle to his middle and fell deeper into his chest, grinding my hips around in these kinky circles like I'd seen Patra and Lady Saw do in reggae videos on Video Music Box. I let my Janet Jackson in *Poetic Justice* braids swing over my shoulders and rubbed my vagina so hard into him something shot straight through me and I just felt my whole inside open up. And I mean literally—from my vagina to my heart. I rubbed harder then and while we were both still in our jeans, as if he hadn't already gotten hard, Ronald's penis grew bigger again and more rigid than anything that should be connected to a human. I abandoned my brain to follow my heart that was begging to feel the thing tickling my middle from the outside in. I am sure I didn't push my hand into Ronald's pants with any elegance. It was more of a shove and grab. I wrapped my hands around his penis and remembered that in seventh grade fast-ass Melissa Montgomery said it should feel like a banana or plantain. I decided that I needed to call Melissa and tell her that either she was wrong or just miscalculating . . . under-calculating. Because what I felt hiding below Ronald's tight abs was more like the long, thick salamis my father used to take the train all the way to this Italian butcher in Bensonhurst to get or one of those long sour pickles from the bodega on the corner near Hamilton Houses.

I don't know if Ronald had ever felt anyone's hands on his penis, gripping it so tightly and fingering it all around slowly like someone trying to confirm that it was real and moving and pulsating to the same rhythm in my hips, but he let out a little sigh, something like an orgasmic moan that sent quakes through the room. He placed his hands on my hips over him and soon his fingers were undoing my zipper.

"You think you're ready for this?" he asked in a whisper that was more confirming than questioning. I don't think I answered. I don't remember answering. Ronald could never recall if I answered. I just started moving. Pulled off my own pants and panties and everything.

I let him enter me while I held my breath and thought of the sounds the A train made when it pulled up at 125th Street (fast-ass Melissa Montgomery's advice). It hurt. It burned like fire. But the more I held my breath and thought of the sounds of the brakes on the subway car screeching against the tracks, the further I left the pain and arrived at something that commanded my every sense like nothing else I'd ever experienced. I couldn't worry about anything. Think about anything. Not my mother. My father. Kent. How we were going to pay for senior year. What I wanted to be when I grew up. At that moment, when Ronald was inside of me, that feeling was all that was on my mind.

I think that was when my brazen undertaking of our love began. How he stole my heart from the outside in. Because after that I was never the same. I was sitting on top of that salami for so long and through so many days and nights skinny Ronald McDonald became a part of me—or maybe I became a part of him (like an appendage). I got a urinary tract infection, a yeast infection, and even popped a muscle in my jaw, but nothing could keep me from that man. I stayed in position on top of him through graduation. Got accepted to Columbia Law *after* he got accepted to NYU Law and started planning our future together. Then *we* were going to be lawyers and *we* were going to save all the poor black people of the world.

Ronald was more than clear on my plans to be with him . . . forever. He said he wanted to be with me. He said I would make a good "mate." After we moved to New York and graduated from law school, he announced that he just needed a little more time on his own to get himself together and then he'd propose. I agreed. Hearing the words *propose* come from his lips at twenty-four was like watching a master chef cook a perfect cut of filet mignon—you'd do anything to taste the final product. Because I lived in adult housing through law school to avoid going home to my father and Kent, I was newly homeless and needed someplace to live quickly. I searched everywhere but I was broke and studying for the bar exam and I couldn't find anything I could afford that wasn't far out in Jersey, damn near upstate or out on Long Island—and again, going home was just out of the question.

One morning my cousin Tamika, who was a booking agent at Wilhelmina Models, said she had a client whose roommate disappeared in the middle of the night. She needed a replacement fast. When I showed up at the rent-controlled two-bedroom loft in Chelsea Piers, this Chinese-looking girl with pecan skin and bushy black hair answered the door in a thin tank top dress. "Please be my new roommate!" she squealed, before even asking my name. "OK," I said quickly. We laughed, sensing our equal desperation. I walked in and then she said her name: Kim. "I'm Kim, too!" I said, like it was such an odd name. "OMG!" she squealed again, so loudly I knew she couldn't be any older than twenty-one and added, "Two Kims! We're the two Kims!" She pulled me to a couch that looked like it had been in the loft since 1905 and proceeded to go over a bunch of stuff about sharing the rent and utilities. There was a neon green bong on the table and a pizza box on the floor near the couch, but I was so busy looking at Kim 2's skin and wondering where she was from and guessing about her parentage that I hardly paid attention to the details of my surroundings. When she asked if I'd be her roommate, I hadn't even heard how much the rent was. "Yes," I said. "I will."

That night I was meeting Ronald for dinner in midtown near his firm and Kim kind of invited herself along. That was her way. She didn't take off the nearly see-through tank-top dress. She slid on some cowgirl boots only a model could get away with and big black shades. She wrapped her arm around mine and asked me to tell her all about Ronald—my soon-to-be-fiancé. I did.

With a mixture of prophetic moments, including an Ecstasy-fueled threesome during year three that apparently continued long after I'd passed out in the hallway, haunting me day and night, it was easy to predict the psychological hell coming five years up the road when my fiancé left me in a hospital emergency room to go comfort my roommate turned best friend.

With that sad moment whirling around in my head, I sat down on the toilet in the bathroom at 44 & X and cried into my hands like a stupid girl. I was done with questions about why it happened and how it happened. I'd been numbed by the whole thing. But seeing Kim and Ronald together, knowing they were obviously still together and eating at my brunch spot brought all of the pain back.

A text came through on my cellphone as I balled up a bunch of toilet paper to wipe my tears. I looked and saw that it was from Kent.

KENT: You coming out of there?

I tried like three times to respond, to say something clear and concise that would hide the full-on breakdown I was having in the stall, like "I'm on my way out" or "Be back in a sec," but nothing would come out right. Then Kent started writing again.

KENT: Come on. Don't let this shit go down with you hiding in the bathroom.

KENT: Hello?

KENT: Kiki Mimi, you better bring your ass out here. Harlem, stand up!

He was trying to make me laugh. I did chuckle a little bit at how stupid he was but I was still sitting on the dirty toilet in hiding and probably earning a bad case of crabs for it.

KENT: Yo, you know how I am. You know I would've dropped this fool on sight behind what he did to you if I really gave a fuck about him. But I ain't do it.

The best thing about being a twin is that sometimes in such a crazy world you know exactly how someone else feels. It's like if Kent is happy or sad, I can actually feel his emotions inside of me. Like they're my own. I felt that when I read Kent's message. I felt his anger. His compassion for my tears. In that moment my little brother was being my big brother again. I texted him back.

ME:Why didn't you fuck him up?

He answered immediately.

KENT: Because this nigga ain't good enough for you.

And then:

KENT: He never was. I was glad when he was gone. If I put my hands on him, he would've thought I gave a fuck. And I didn't. And I wanted him to know that. Man-to-man. He wasn't good enough.

I can't say my tears went from sad to happy. That would be a full exaggeration. It's more accurate to say Kent made me smile. Made me a little tougher.

I wiped my tears one last time and flushed the tissue down the toilet. I straightened my back and walked out of the stall with the full intention of returning to the table, finishing my brunch, and moving on . . . again.

When I was in the mirror cleaning streaks of mascara from my cheeks, Kent sent more texts:

KENT: Yo, you coming out? I paid the bill, so we can leave as soon as you walk out.

KENT: Yo?

ME: Yes. I'm coming out now.

I felt the phone vibrate again when I was stuffing it back into my purse, but I knew it was probably just Kent again, so I ignored it and went to walk out of the bathroom.

I took one of those deep, courage begging breaths and pulled the bathroom door open.

And then standing right there in front of me was Kim 2.

I was so not prepared for that. I'm saying, if I had been, I would've said some slick Erica Kane-like line that cut her down at the knees and threatened her life. But a good line or practiced uppercut was so far from my mind, I just tried to walk past her. I didn't even roll my eyes.

She put her cold hand on my arm and my first reaction was to pull away.

But she grabbed me again.

"No, just wait," she said, trying to get ahold of me.

"Wait? What?" I threw my arms up to escape her. "Don't touch me. Don't fucking touch me."

She reached again and I jumped back.

"Kim, stop. I just want to say—"

"I don't want to talk to you. I don't want to hear what you have to say. I've told you that so many times. Just stop," I said, repeating sentiments I'd sent in response to the many e-mails and texts Kim had sent me after her relationship with my fiancé came to light. They had been a couple, an actual couple, for over a year. She'd met his parents. They'd gone to the Poconos together—all of this while I was with him.

"I just want you to hear me out," she said.

"Hear what? I don't need to hear anything I don't already know. You stole my fiancé. You said you were my best friend, but meanwhile, you were sleeping with my man behind my back."

"We both know that's not how it went down. You guys were—"

"That's how I know the story and that's all I care to know," I said. "I'm not one of those people who need to know why. Your motives were obvious. You wanted him from the start. You knew how much I loved him, how much he loved me, but you wanted him for yourself anyway. We were supposed to get married."

"You didn't have a ring. He never even asked you."

"So?"

"So. . . . Look, none of it was done on purpose," Kim said. "It just happened. I swear."

"You can tell that bullshit to someone else," I shot back, "someone who wasn't nearly killed in a car your high ass was driving."

"We both know I never meant for that to happen. You—you—"

"Really? Well explain how when I was in surgery you were fucking calling Ronald to get you out of jail. Explain how when I was laid up in bed in the hospital and the doctors thought I might be paralyzed from the neck down you never once came to see me and you moved out of the apartment we were sharing and in with Ronald. Explain that. Did you mean for all of that to happen? Or was all of that a surprise to you too? Because it was certainly a fucking surprise to me."

I didn't realize I was hollering at Kim, had my finger pointed at the little space between her eyebrows like a .22 threatening to lick a shot until I felt all of the eyes in the restaurant on me. I turned to see that a little crowd was gathered and right in front were Kent and Ronald.

I slowly lowered my hand and tried to rediscover my sensible mind where my anger for being disbarred and losing my job for beating Kim's ass in my favorite restaurant would outweigh the joy I'd feel after I choked her to death. And I think she was waiting for it too, because she was quiet and while my hands had been up before, now she was standing there with her hands raised like I was about to arrest her.

"You know what, don't explain a damn thing," I said. "Because, as I said, I don't give a fuck."

I'd finally found my Erica Kane line, and it was weak at best, but I tossed my purse over my arm and walked right into the crowd where Kent and Ronald were waiting.

I got to Ronald first and when he opened his mouth to say God only knows what to me, I put my hand up to stop him.

"Don't say anything to me," I shot. "Nothing."

Kent grabbed me and pulled me out of the restaurant as I went through a list of other things I needed to say that I probably should've kept to myself.

"I sent you a text when she got up. Told you she was coming into the bathroom," Kent said after I'd stumbled out behind him. "You OK?"

He pulled me around the corner and pushed me up against the side of a building.

"I'm fine. I'm fine."

"I was trying to get you out of there. I kept texting you."

"I know. The phone was in my purse."

Kent's fists were balled at his sides like he was about to fight someone.

"I was about to drop that motherfucker," he fired. "If I wasn't with you and shit, I would've stomped his ass out. But I know how you get down, so I tried to keep cool."

I don't know how I found the comedy, but I actually started laughing. And loudly.

"What? What are you laughing at?" Kent asked, looking like he was about to run back around the corner to fight Ronald.

"I don't know. I just," I started, "I guess it's funny how you said you didn't fight him before because he wasn't good enough for me, but now you're all riled up and ready to throw down."

Kent rolled his eyes and sucked his teeth.

"Look at you," I went on still laughing.

"Yeah, whatever. You better be glad you're a lawyer and I knew the last thing you wanted was for some nigga shit to go down in there, because we were both about to be rumbling—sister and brother."

"Really?"

"I can't have that fool getting my Kiki Mimi all upset and hiding in a bathroom. Mess up my rep in these streets. Have niggas thinking I'm soft."

I put my arms out and pulled Kent into a hug.

"Maybe you're just soft enough. Soft enough to save me," I said and I felt happiness wash over my twin brother.

"Ohh," Kent said. "Well how about you save me, too?"

"What? How?" I asked. I'd already forgotten about what he'd asked me at the table.

"Lydia. My fiancée. Your sister-in-law. Pull some strings. Make some calls!" Kent backed up so I could see his begging smile.

"Ahhh, to that I still say no. Not even in a million years Kent. No. And hell no. Nice smile though."